Rebecca Greenwood has ʼ
that will set people free f.
plagued them. She opens closed doors and releases the light
of hope into areas that keep people in bondage to difficult
issues such as depression, fear, rejection, unbelief, confusion,
and other strongholds of the mind.

—CINDY JACOBS
COFOUNDER, GENERALS INTERNATIONAL

In every generation there are new voices who arise and
whom God appoints and anoints. Rebecca Greenwood is
such a person for such a time as this. Her teachings are bib-
lically solid, piercing with truth yet laced in grace; highly
spiritual and yet amazingly practical. The battle is won or
lost at the threshold of the mind. This book will help you
to win your battle and equip you to help deliver others.
Remember, you shall know the truth and the truth shall set
you free!

—JAMES W. GOLL
PRESIDENT, ENCOUNTERS NETWORK
BEST-SELLING AUTHOR, THE SEER AND
THE LOST ART OF INTERCESSION

This book is a wonderful new tool, both for deliverance
ministers and for those struggling with emotional issues or
mental battles. The mind is often an intense playground that
the devil invades to keep people from a victorious life of
freedom in Christ. But glorious freedom from torment is
possible, and this book clearly explains how that can happen.

—DORIS M. WAGNER
MINISTER AND VICE PRESIDENT, GLOBAL SPHERES CENTER

Many believers have experienced adversity and spiritual battles in their minds and emotions. Truthfully, we are not to
let negative thoughts or emotions rule us and open the door

to fear or insecurity. Instead we are to rein in these thoughts through the power of the salvation and wholeness we have received through Christ. God's light of faithfulness is able to shine through the debris from past seasons and cause us to rise in freedom because it is our nature to overcome. In this book Rebecca Greenwood provides the spiritual, scriptural, and practical tools that will empower us to lay hold of the freedom we have in Christ and live victoriously.

—DUTCH SHEETS
PRAYER LEADER AND AUTHOR OF THE BEST SELLER
INTERCESSORY PRAYER

Excellent! Powerful! Needed for every believer! Rebecca Greenwood exposits the means and the ways of experiencing the fullness of our victory in Christ Jesus.

—JACK GREENWOOD
PASTOR, HOPE COMMUNITY CHURCH
MARLOW, OKLAHOMA

DEFEATING STRONGHOLDS
of the MIND

REBECCA GREENWOOD

CHARISMA
HOUSE

Most CHARISMA HOUSE BOOK GROUP products are available at special quantity discounts for bulk purchase for sales promotions, premiums, fund-raising, and educational needs. For details, write Charisma House Book Group, 600 Rinehart Road, Lake Mary, Florida 32746, or telephone (407) 333-0600.

DEFEATING STRONGHOLDS OF THE MIND
   by Rebecca Greenwood
Published by Charisma House
Charisma Media/Charisma House Book Group
600 Rinehart Road
Lake Mary, Florida 32746
www.charismahouse.com

This book or parts thereof may not be reproduced in any form, stored in a retrieval system, or transmitted in any form by any means—electronic, mechanical, photocopy, recording, or otherwise—without prior written permission of the publisher, except as provided by United States of America copyright law.

Unless otherwise noted, all Scripture quotations are from the Holy Bible, New International Version®, NIV®. Copyright © 1973, 1978, 1984, 2011 by Biblica, Inc.™ Used by permission of Zondervan. All rights reserved worldwide. www.zondervan.com. The "NIV" and "New International Version" are trademarks registered in the United States Patent and Trademark Office by Biblica, Inc.™

Scripture quotations marked AMP are from the Amplified Bible. Copyright © 1954, 1958, 1962, 1964, 1965, 1987 by The Lockman Foundation. Used by permission.

Scripture quotations marked ASV are from the American Standard Bible.

Scripture quotations marked KJV are from the King James Version of the Bible.

Scripture quotations marked MEV are taken from the Modern English Version. Copyright © 2014 by Military Bible Association. Used by permission. All rights reserved.

Scripture quotations marked NAS are from the New American Standard Bible, copyright © 1960, 1962, 1963, 1968, 1971, 1972, 1973, 1975, 1977, 1995 by The Lockman Foundation. Used by permission. (www.Lockman.org)

Scripture quotations marked NKJV are from the New King James Version®. Copyright © 1982 by Thomas Nelson. Used by permission. All rights reserved.

Scripture quotations marked THE MESSAGE are from *The Message: The Bible in Contemporary English*, copyright © 1993, 1994, 1995, 1996, 2000, 2001, 2002. Used by permission of NavPress Publishing Group.

Scripture quotations marked TLB are from The Living Bible. Copyright © 1971. Used by permission of Tyndale House Publishers, Inc., Wheaton, IL 60189. All rights reserved.

Unless otherwise noted, all Greek and Hebrew definitions are taken from Libronix Digital Library System (Oak Harbor, WA: Libronix Corporation, 2000-2001), specifically J. Strong, *Enhanced Strong's Lexicon* (Bellingham, WA: Logos Bible Software, 1996) and J. Swanson, *Dictionary of Biblical Languages With Semitic Domains: Greek (New Testament)* (Bellingham, WA: Logos Bible Software, 1997).

While all the accounts described in this book are true, some examples are composites created by the author from her experiences in ministry. Names and details of their stories have been changed, and any similarity between the names and stories of individuals described in this book to individuals known to readers is purely coincidental.

Copyright © 2015 by Rebecca Greenwood
All rights reserved

Cover design by Justin Evans

Visit the author's website at www.christianharvestintl.org.

Library of Congress Cataloging-in-Publication Data:
Greenwood, Rebecca, 1967-
   Defeating strongholds of the mind / by Rebecca Greenwood. -- First edition.
      pages cm
   Includes bibliographical references.
   ISBN 978-1-62136-988-2 (trade paper) -- ISBN 978-1-62136-989-9 (e-book)
   1. Thought and thinking--Religious aspects--Christianity. 2. Spiritual warfare. I. Title.
   BV4598.4.G75 2015
   248.4--dc23
                                        2014041696

First edition

15 16 17 18 19 — 987654321
Printed in the United States of America

DEDICATION

I dedicate this book to our three committed I-1 intercessors, Flora Veneskey, Joyce Nicodin, and Rebecca Ontiveros. You three are priceless jewels to Greg, the girls, our ministry, and me. Thank you for your tireless hours of intercession and commitment to us. I am forever grateful to each of you and love you dearly.

CONTENTS

ACKNOWLEDGMENTS

THERE ARE MANY individuals to whom I would like to express my sincere gratitude for aiding me in the process of completing this manuscript. As I type, I joyfully and in amusement remember a key conversation I engaged in not so many years ago. I approached Peter Wagner and in total innocence asked, "Peter, what do you do when you have received five prophetic words to write a book?" His reply, "What do you mean, what do you do? It's simple. You write the book!"

At that time I had no idea how to write a book. Eleven years later, I sit writing this acknowledgments page, marking the completion of my seventh writing project. God amazes me at His supernatural ability to get us on the right track in our spiritual walk. Thank you, Peter, for being the voice of influence in my life, for pushing me out of the nest, for encouraging me to write, and for helping me discover a strategic gifting and anointing in my spiritual calling.

To my husband, Greg. We did it again! Woohoo! We made it through another eight-month season of writing, researching, praying, midnight-hour prophetic downloads, and my asking for your guidance and wisdom all along the way. I love you and thank God every day for you.

To our three beautiful daughters, thank you for the incredible patience and understanding you exhibit when I am in book-writing mode and for your invaluable input to ensure that I include topics that will impact many in your generation. Your father and I are so proud of you and are blessed to be your parents. You inspire me!

Brandon and Kate Larson, you guys ever amaze me at

your faithfulness to read my manuscripts as I am creatively birthing. Your friendship and input are greatly valued and appreciated. Maureen Eha, thank you for believing in me as a minister and as an author.

Jayde and Christy Duncan and our Antioch church family, Greg and I love you! Your belief and partnership has meant the world to us. We are so grateful to have a church family to journey with that believes and accepts our calling and gifting to deliverance, intercessory prayer, warfare prayer, and prophecy.

Larry and Marilyn Davis, I say this all the time in public but I want to put it in writing: thank you for the awesome job you are doing in running the deliverance and inner-healing focus of our ministry. You truly are a gift to us.

And to all of you who have sought us for help in deliverance ministry and prayer over the past twenty-two years, thank you for the privilege of allowing us to journey with you in seeing the Lord set you free. As I reminisce about all those beautiful moments of God's delivering love and power, I am moved to tears. So many lives transfigured into His awesome freedom. What an honor to walk in this calling.

And to Jesus, my Savior, my friend, the lover of my soul—my everything. Thank You for coming into that room as I was walking the fence between a lifestyle of rebellion and one of commitment and holiness and for completely capturing my heart and life. You are truly magnificent. I love You.

FOREWORD

THE PROFESSOR'S VOICE was drowned out as my heart began to beat louder. My stomach knotted up, and my clenched fists began to sweat. The thought of the history final was daunting to me. Not to mention that there was an essay portion of the exam. As my legs shook under my chair, I kept repeating in my mind, "You have the mind of Christ; you're more than a conqueror. I can do all things through Christ who strengthens me."

It's no secret that throughout high school and into my early college years I struggled with academics. I joke now that I had to cheat on my tests just to get Cs. Unlike my studious older sister and my intelligent younger brother, I was the "middle child" and found myself struggling to maintain average grades. I often labeled myself as "dumb," "lazy," and "slow." In fact, those word curses I told myself started to become a reality early on in my childhood. I told myself that I couldn't take tests, that I wasn't smart enough, and that therefore, I was a failure.

However, when I first became a Christian, I was radically changed. God instantly delivered me from drugs, and my lifestyle quickly turned around. That meant no more cheating in school. I knew that the Lord was calling me to holiness and consecration, and part of that journey meant digging deep into the Word. I spent hours a day memorizing Scripture, studying the Bible, and reading through chapters at a time. I was hungry for the Lord and His Word. I was literally renewing my mind daily by speaking the blessings, promises, and truth of God over my life.

As I continued the daily devotion of memorizing the

Bible, something beautiful and miraculous began to happen. The Lord literally began to restore my mind! My grades shifted dramatically to As as I declared the Word of God: "I am a new creation—the old has passed. I am made in the image of God." I was no longer bound to the lie that I was a bad test-taker, slow, and a poor student. Through the memorization of Scripture and the renewing of my mind, God showed me who I really was as a son!

The power of the cross is not just for the salvation of our sins. God intended for us to live life in wholeness on earth as in heaven—to be strengthened in our mind, will, and emotions here and now. Rebecca Greenwood addresses this war that goes on in our minds. Sometimes it takes more than a heart transformation—it takes the renewing of our minds. Proverbs 23:7 states that as a man "thinks within himself, so he is" (NAS). The truth is, what we think on is what we believe and, in time, what we become. Rebecca goes into detail about the strongholds of the mind and how they affect our attitudes, actions, and emotions. Our lives can be changed if we shift our thinking!

Rebecca's book skillfully outlines what strongholds are so that you can help identify any in your own life. My prayer for you is that the Holy Spirit unlocks the strongholds in your own life so that you can start living life to the fullest!

—Dr. Ché Ahn
Senior pastor, HRock Church,
Pasadena, California
President, Harvest International Ministry
International Chancellor,
Wagner Leadership Institute

INTRODUCTION

I F YOU WERE just tougher and would man up, girls would like you, and everyone would think you were cool!" Sighing, Dan closed his eyes and attempted to silence the familiar lie that had repeated itself in his mind since his freshman year in high school. "When will this battle end? After all, I'm almost thirty years old," he whispered wearily as he rubbed his hand across his forehead in an attempt to silence his mind. The unfortunate cause of this torment was the persistent teasing Dan had encountered from his older brother and his peers throughout his high-school years. He had grown up in a small town where boys were expected to get involved in sports. His gifting, however, was in music and drama, which made Dan the object of ridicule.

This accusatory lie that his brother and his peers repeated for years had so gripped Dan's beliefs about himself that a stronghold of rejection had taken root in his mind, and he continually felt that he was inadequate as a man and as a husband. As a result, after five years of marriage, an increasing emotional distance grew between him and his wife, Sarah. One Sunday afternoon it was clear from the hurt and confusion in Sarah's eyes that the tension in their marriage, caused by Dan's sense of inadequacy, had reached a crucial point. Dan prayed in earnest, "God, help me overcome this lie. Show me how to defeat this stronghold in my mind."

That night Dan attended the Sunday night service at his church. God in His faithfulness brought an answer to his prayer. As the speaker made her way to the platform, Dan could feel the presence and peace of God begin to rest on him. As the speaker prepared to share, she opened in prayer,

"Lord, we welcome You to the service tonight. Holy Spirit, come and minister to each person in this room. Help these individuals to recognize the lies and the battles that are raging in their minds, and let this be their day of freedom and victory." As Dan listened to the message of how to defeat strongholds of the mind, he fought back tears. At the end of the message, he quickly made his way to the front.

Kneeling at the altar, he prayed, "Lord, forgive me for believing the lies of rejection that others have falsely spoken over me and that the enemy has established as a stronghold in my mind. Lord, I choose right now to forgive my brother and my friends who persistently teased me. Forgive me for entertaining the lies of this stronghold and for the walls of protection I have built around my heart and emotions to keep people away, especially my wife. I declare that I will no longer believe the lie that I am not tough enough or that I am an inadequate man. I speak to the stronghold in my mind and emotions to be silent now, in Jesus's name. Lord, I know that You make no mistakes. Your Word says that I am fearfully and wonderfully made. Thank You for Your healing love. I welcome Your healing touch. Let it flood over and through my mind and emotions."

With tears of joy rolling down his cheeks, Dan smiled as the Lord's love and holiness brought tangible freedom to his thoughts. He felt as if a heavy burden was being lifted off his mind. A newfound love for the Lord and for his wife flooded his mind and heart. A yearning for reading God's Word was birthed in him. In order to maintain his victory, Dan committed to reading the Bible every day. Before long he realized that he was no longer angry when he thought about his brother and his friends. He no longer rehearsed the lie of inadequacy, and the truths of God's Word filled his thoughts. Healing and happiness came to his marriage, as his wife, Sarah, happily testified: "I have a new husband!"

YOU TOO CAN HAVE
LIFE-CHANGING VICTORY!

A stronghold of the mind is a lie that Satan establishes in our thinking. It is a statement that we count as true but that is actually false. Jesus said we have an evil and deceptive enemy: "There is no truth in him. When he lies, he speaks his native language, for he is a liar and the father of lies" (John 8:44). Satan is a liar who wages warfare against God's children. One of his tactics is mental warfare whereby, over time, he causes a battle to rage in our mind that keeps us feeling accused and intimidated. It is no mistake that he is called the "accuser of our brethren" (Rev. 12:10, NKJV). He uses false guilt and tormenting thoughts to remind us of our past failures, or he speaks lies against us in an attempt to cripple or devastate our Christian walk. He will invade our thought life, causing us to embrace wrong thinking, bad attitudes, and emotional scars.

This is what was happening to Dan. He was battling a stronghold of the mind. Even though the lie had been spoken by others, it had become such a source of torment in his thought life that Dan truly believed he was an inadequate man. His true kingdom identity, his marriage, and his future were at stake.

John 8:32 teaches us, "You will know the truth, and the truth will set you free." God desires that each of His children walk in victory and freedom in every area of their lives. It is not just truth that sets us free but *knowing* the truth that sets us free. When we as children of God know the truth and understand that we can be delivered from unhealthy emotions and victorious over wrong thinking, we are empowered to partner with the Lord to claim our victory. We can then become independent from the lies of darkness, the strongholds of our minds, and our wounded emotions. We can learn to control our thoughts and to think on good things, on the goodness of God, and on His Word. We can praise and exalt the Lord and, as a result, disarm the enemy and find life-changing freedom. The good news is that Dan heard the truth, repented for believing a lie, and forgave those who had hurt him. He welcomed God's healing touch and set his mind on the truths of God's Word. His life was dramatically transformed as a result!

Maybe this story sounds familiar to you. If so, I am glad you are reading this book. As we discovered with Dan, identifying the root of wrong beliefs and strongholds of the mind can be life-changing. We can change our lives by changing our thinking. God's Word teaches us that we are to be renewed in our minds so that we can think the way God thinks. When this occurs, we will experience a life over-flowing with the fruit of the Spirit—a life full of kingdom purpose, joy, peace, faithfulness, and freedom. A whole new world will be opened up to us, one in which we will learn to choose our own thoughts and to forbid the enemy from filling our minds with thoughts that defeat us.

It is my prayer that this book will not only instruct you but will bless you with freedom! I pray that a desire for personal encounters with our magnificent Lord will arise in you and that those encounters will burn the dross out of your thoughts and emotions. Whether you are a new believer or one who has walked with the Lord for many years, I pray that you will be empowered to take responsibility for your thoughts; see the strongholds of your mind defeated; and experience peace of mind, healthy thoughts, and the full-ness of abundant joy and freedom that are made available to us through Jesus Christ.

Chapter 1

HOLY SPIRIT, DOES MY
MIND NEED FREEDOM?

Therefore, my dear ones, as you have always obeyed [my suggestions], so now, not only [with the enthusiasm you would show] in my presence but much more because I am absent, work out (cultivate, carry out to the goal, and fully complete) your own salvation with reverence and awe and trembling (self-distrust, with serious caution, tenderness of conscience, watchfulness against temptation, timidly shrinking from whatever might offend God and discredit the name of Christ).

[PHILIPPIANS 2:12, AMP]

NONE OF US are excused from the need to overcome wrong beliefs, thought patterns, and strongholds that have gripped our mind and emotions. As the verse at the opening of the chapter indicates, we are to work out our salvation. The Greek word translated *work out* in the verse means "something done with thoroughness." To work something out means to undergo a complete, through-and-through process in order to attain to a desired finished work. Meanwhile, the Greek word for *salvation* is translated "deliverance, preservation, safety, and salvation." Putting this all together we see that salvation, which the apostle Paul tells us we are to "work out," is an intentional personal process of becoming more and more Christlike. This is to take place not only in our actions but also in our thoughts and emotions. But, unfortunately, I believe our thought life is often the last place in which we gain victory in our lives.

Proverbs 23:7 tells us, "For as he thinks in his heart, so is he" (AMP). The word *thinks* here indicates that whatever we believe about ourselves, we are. I can totally relate to this scripture, as I am sure can many others. As I grow in my Christian walk and minister to people all around the world, it is evident to me that what we think and what we say are of great importance. The truth is, what we think on is what we believe and, in time, what we become. Our thought lives are the pioneers that lead the way to what will play out in our lives personally, emotionally, and spiritually. What we dwell on will even influence how we step into God's plan for our lives.

Interestingly, researchers are confirming the scriptural truth in Proverbs:

> Negative thinking slows down brain coordination, making it difficult to process thoughts and find solutions. Feeling frightened, which often happens when focused on negative outcomes, has been shown to decrease activity in your cerebellum, which slow the brain's ability to process new information—limiting your ability to practice creative problem solving. Additionally, the fear factor impacts your left temporal lobe, which affects mood, memory, and impulse control.
>
> Your frontal lobe, particularly your PFC [prefrontal cortex], decides what is important according to the amount of attention you pay to something and how you feel about it. Thus, the more you focus on negativity, the more synapses and neurons your brain will create that support your negative thought process.
>
> Your hippocampus provides the context of stored memories, which means the emotional tone and description your mind creates can potentially rewire your brain by creating stronger neuronal pathways and synapses. What you think and feel about a certain situation or thing can become so deeply ingrained that you will have to work hard to dismantle the negative connections and rewire your brain in order to be less

afraid, to think positively, to believe that dreams can come true, to trust that your efforts will be successful.[1]

SETTING OUR MINDS

Romans 8:5 says, "Those who are according to the flesh and are controlled by its unholy desires set their minds on and pursue those things which gratify the flesh, but those who are according to the Spirit and are controlled by the desires of the Spirit set their minds on and seek those things which gratify the [Holy] Spirit" (AMP). To *set our mind* means "to view, hold belief in, honor or acknowledge with high status an opinion of one's self." Basically, what we choose to set our minds on and to think about will determine our actions as we maneuver through life.

When we spend time with an individual, we learn the focus of that person's thought life. How do we do this? By listening to the words that come out of the person's mouth and observing his or her actions and emotional condition. This is also how we can learn to discern the focus of our own thoughts. If we think on negative things, we will begin to see the fruit of those negative thoughts in our lives. But if we think and believe on good thoughts—on the Word of God and on His promises for our lives—we will become living examples of His truths.

For the last year I have trained to run a 5K race with my oldest daughter. A year ago I never would have believed that I could jog 3.1 miles without stopping. To be truthful, I would have thought the idea laughable. But I do love a new challenge, and my oldest daughter, understanding this, issued the invitation, "Come on, Mom, I challenge you to begin training. In a few months you and I can enter a 5K. We can do it together. It will be fun!"

Oddly enough, and to my surprise, I felt the Lord nudging me to change—to redirect my beliefs concerning myself and to embrace this new challenge. A year later, my daughter and I ran our first 5K. It turns out that the training process leading up to the race was not only good for my physical body, but also good for my thought life.

I quickly learned that accomplishing my workouts depended on my thoughts. "You have no business doing this. You're forty-six years old. You're out of shape, and you don't like jogging. You can never do this." I had to learn to think on what I was able to accomplish and on the Word of God! Often, while I'm out jogging these days, I can be heard saying, "I can do all things through Christ who strengthens me. I can go farther. I can make it another quarter of a mile. I speak to my mind to believe that I can do this." The more I have voiced this and told myself to listen and believe, the stronger I have grown and the more my thoughts have changed.

DO YOU BELIEVE GOD WANTS TO HEAL YOUR MIND?

So many people surrender to a life of victory and freedom because they are unable to relate to the Father's heart of love that our God so graciously extends to us. Sadly, many of these people have lived through negative experiences with their earthly fathers and mothers. Some may have grown up in homes with no affection or with absentee parents. Others may have endured emotionally, physically, or verbally abusive situations. Some may have suffered from living with addicts, sexual abuse, or bullying.

Not only are each of these scenarios a devastating picture of the fallen world, but they also explain why fear and apprehension often exist in people's relationships—even their relationship with the heavenly Father, who lavishes nothing but love on us. Those who have experienced this kind of pain have difficulty believing they are loved sons and daughters of God. Oftentimes they feel orphaned and separate from their true kingdom inheritance.

The beautiful thing is, God created each of us *because* He has a Father's heart, and He desired a family of His own. He wanted sons and daughters to relate to. He loves each and every one of us with a love greater than we can even fathom, a love that is never ending—so much so that He gave His only Son to die on the cross to make atonement for our sins so that we could be set free from the dominion of sin and darkness and be with Him forever.

John the beloved apostle put it this way: "See what great love the Father has lavished on us, that we should be called children of God! And that is what we are! The reason the world does not know us is that it did not know him" (1 John 3:1). The word for *love* in this verse is *agape,* and it refers to an abundance of love—a love feast. It is an extravagant love that is without end. It captures the deepest aspect of God's nature—He *is* love.

I have discovered that once we experience the Father's heart of love, the encounter leaves us longing for more. God is a holy, compassionate, merciful, slow-to-anger, loving, kind, faithful Father. He created each of us in a specific way and has plans for each of our lives. He is a good God, and every one of us matters greatly to Him. He wants you and me to walk in an assurance of His great love and to love Him with great abandonment. Jesus teaches the importance of love in Mark 12:28–30:

> One of the scribes came and heard them reasoning together. Perceiving that Jesus had answered them well, he asked Him, "Which is the first command-ment of all?" Jesus answered him, "The first of all the commandments is, 'Hear, O Israel, the Lord our God is one Lord. You shall love the Lord your God with all your heart, and with all your soul, and with all

your mind, and with all your strength.' This is the
first commandment."

—MEV

It is from this place of loving the Father and receiving
His love for us that we are able to love ourselves and others.
It is here that we are empowered to become and to walk in
all that God has destined for us. And it is in this place that
we are positioned to recognize areas in our thoughts and
beliefs that need the Father's healing and delivering touch.

DECEPTION IS SUBTLE

We often think that when we encounter evil or deception
it will be as obvious as Satan standing in front of us with a
pitchfork in hand and horns on his head. But actually, the
lies and deceit of the enemy, the world, and our own flesh
will be more subtle than that. When Satan tempted Eve to
sin in the garden, he did not forthrightly say, "God was
wrong. You *can* eat from the tree of knowledge of good and
evil. Don't listen to Him; listen to me! Come on. Disobey
what God said to you!" That would have been a blatant, in-
your-face red flag for Adam and Eve.

The enemy was much more subtle in order to cause Eve to
question and doubt what she already knew to be true. Let's look
at the dialogue that transpired between the serpent and Eve:

> Now the serpent was more subtle than any beast of
> the field which the Lord God had made. And he said
> to the woman, "Has God said, 'You shall not eat of
> any tree of the garden'?"
>
> —GENESIS 3:1, MEV

Here we see Satan subtly challenge the truth of God's
word in such a way that Eve began to question what God
had spoken to her. Eve responded with truth and defended
God's direction:

We may eat of the fruit from the trees of the garden;
but from the fruit of the tree which is in the midst of
the garden, God has said, "You will not eat of it, nor
will you touch it, or else you will die."

—GENESIS 3:2–3, MEV

Satan, in a patient pursuit to trap his victim, again slyly
countered the truth of God's guidance: "You surely will not
die! For God knows that on the day you eat of it your eyes
will be opened and you will be like God, knowing good
and evil" (Gen. 3:4–5, MEV). Satan was luring Eve into an
encounter in which she in her human nature—that place
in our created being where God has gifted each of us with
self-will—would desire to become like God and to decide
for herself what she would do and believe. We all know
the outcome. Satan succeeded, and Eve, followed by Adam,
"exchanged the truth about God for a lie" (Rom. 1:25).

From years of experience ministering freedom to others, I
can confidently say that most of the issues in our lives begin
with a subtle deception that leads to a spirit of compromise.
This deception and compromise birth a demonic lie about
God that we come to believe. This usually begins as a slow
deception that over time becomes a stronghold. Getting us
to think wrongly about God is crucial to the enemy's plan,
because what we believe about God will inevitably determine our beliefs about ourselves, others, and the situations
in our lives, as well as determine our emotional condition,
attitudes, and actions.

Because all lies about God come from Satan, whenever
we entertain these lies, they become open doors for strongholds to be established in our minds. Let's investigate
another scriptural example in which subtle lies and wrong
thinking made for difficult circumstances.

THE LIMITS OF JONAH'S BELIEFS

Many of us are familiar with the story of Jonah. For the sake of time and space I will paraphrase it. He was a prophet called and sent by God to proclaim a message to Nineveh, a city steeped in sin. At this time Nineveh was an enemy of Israel. Even so, the Lord sent Jonah to deliver a message to its people that could possibly cause them to turn from their evil ways.

Jonah quickly disobeyed and headed in the opposite direction of Nineveh, taking a ship to Tarshish. Because of his disobedience, the Lord caused a great storm, endangering the ship and all the sailors. The men on the ship began to cry out to their gods for deliverance, while Jonah descended into the lower parts of the ship and fell fast asleep. When the captain located Jonah, he urged him to call on his God that the Lord might rescue them, but Jonah did not oblige. The mariners decided to cast lots in order to discover who had brought about this calamity. The Lord caused the lot to fall on Jonah. Being found out, Jonah convinced the mariners to throw him overboard, because he knew that his disobedience had caused this storm.

Once Jonah was thrown overboard, the storm ceased, and the Lord sent a whale to swallow Jonah in order to transport him to the correct location and deliver him onto dry land. After three days, Jonah prayed and was delivered from the belly of the great fish. Needless to say, he now chose obedience to the Lord and delivered the prophetic message to the city of Nineveh: "Forty more days and Nineveh will be overturned" (Jon. 3:4)! In response, the people and the king of Nineveh cried out to God. The Lord relented and did not bring the calamity on Nineveh that He had spoken through Jonah.

> Jonah was displeased and angry. He prayed, saying:
> He prayed to the LORD and said, "O LORD! Is this not
> what I said while I was still in my own land? This is

the reason that I fled before to Tarshish, because I knew that You are a gracious God and merciful, slow to anger, abundant in faithfulness, and ready to relent from punishment. Therefore, Lord, take my life from me, for it is better for me to die than to live."

—JONAH 4:2–3, MEV

Jonah rejected the goodness God wanted to show the Ninevites. Actually, his attitude symbolized the condition of the nation of Israel at this point in history. His self-interest was illustrative of Israel's lack of concern for the ways and mercies of God. Jonah's thinking was in contrast to God's compassion. The literal translation of the word *anger* used to describe Jonah in Jonah 4:1 is "became hot." To put it mildly, Jonah was furious that God spared Nineveh, and it stemmed from an unbalanced patriotic fervor. Jonah probably knew from the prophets Amos and Hosea that Assyria would be Israel's destroyer.

Out of wrong thinking, anger, and disgust, the prophet rebuked his Lord, saying, in essence, "I know that You are forgiving—and now look what has happened!" Jonah admitted that he had fled toward Tarshish because he did not want the Ninevites to be saved from judgment. While in the belly of the whale, Jonah wanted his own deliverance from calamity (Jon. 2:2, 7), but he did not want the Ninevites to be kept from disaster.

The Ninevites were more ready to accept God's grace than Jonah was for them to receive it. Jonah, who had received God's compassion, had no compassion for Nineveh's people. You see, he knew that God was willing to forgive, but he did not want his enemies to know it. He knew that God was gracious, compassionate, slow to anger, and abounding in love. That part he had right. But in the deceptive subtlety of the stronghold in Jonah's mind, he feared what would happen if all these attributes of God were extended toward the despicable, cruel Ninevites.

Jonah's anguish over what God did for Nineveh led him to request that he might die (Jon. 4:8), though earlier he had prayed to live (Jon. 2:2). Perhaps Jonah was struggling with thoughts of embarrassment because the prophecy he delivered had not been carried out. Jonah was so distraught that God had relented of His wrath and had not destroyed the city, he lost all reason for living. God was concerned about the city, but Jonah was not.

Even though Jonah knew that God was slow to anger, he still wanted the Lord to execute His wrath swiftly. Yet God, hesitant to be angry even with His prophet, sought to reason with Jonah. God asked the sulking messenger whether his anger was justified (Jon. 4:4). This question implied that Jonah had no right to be angry.

Jonah was so distraught that he did not answer God. Instead, he left the city, built a crude shelter, and sat down where he could have a clear view of Nineveh. Why he waited to see what would happen to the city is difficult to understand. Maybe he thought God would grant his desire and judge the city anyway. Unable to imagine God not carrying out His justice on people who deserved it, Jonah was determined to wait until Nineveh was in fact judged. But he thought wrongly, and his action was childish. Obviously he had forgotten that he, who also deserved death for disobedience, had been graciously and mercifully delivered by God.

God, in His Father's heart of mercy, began to work on Jonah's wrong thinking that Nineveh should not receive any mercy and his resulting anger. As Jonah sat and awaited Nineveh's outcome, the Lord provided a plant to shade him from the intense heat, which pleased Jonah. But then the Lord prepared a worm to eat the plant, which withered and died:

When the sun rose, God appointed a scorching east wind, and the sun beat upon the head of Jonah so that he became faint and asked that he might die. He said, "It is better for me to die than to live."

Then God said to Jonah, "Is it right for you to be angry about the plant?"

And Jonah replied, "It is right for me to be angry, even to death."

—JONAH 4:8–9, MEV

Let's keep reading so we can learn from the Lord's response:

The LORD said, "You are troubled about the plant for which you did not labor and did not grow. It came up in a night and perished in a night. Should I not, therefore, be concerned about Nineveh, that great city, in which there are more than a hundred and twenty thousand people, who do not know their right hand from their left, and also many animals?"

—JONAH 4:10–11, MEV

To paraphrase God's response to Jonah: "Let's examine this anger of yours, Jonah. It represents your concern over your beloved plant, but what did the plant really mean to you? Your attachment to it couldn't be very deep, for it was here one day and gone the next. Your concern was dictated by thoughts of self-interest, not by genuine love. You never had the devotion of a gardener. If you feel as bad as you do, how would you expect a gardener to feel if he had tended a plant and watched it grow only to see it wither and die? This is how I feel about Nineveh, only much more strongly. I made all those people and all those animals. I created them and have cherished them all these years. Nineveh has cost Me much time and effort. Your pain is nothing compared to Mine when I consider their destruction." Jonah had thought God was illogical in sparing the Assyrians, but God exposed Jonah as the one whose thinking was deceptive, self-focused, and childish.

This story of Jonah is an eye-opening illustration of how a stronghold of the mind can result in wrong actions, attitudes, emotions, and rebellion against God. For some of us, the battle in our mind is hidden; therefore many around us are unaware of our private war. For others of us, much as we saw with Jonah, the strongholds in our minds have gained such a foothold that we act out in our attitudes and actions the sinful fruit of the evil lies.

We need to realize, of course, that sometimes a problem we are dealing with is not a stronghold. Sometimes it is a character issue or a personality weakness that we must intentionally choose to correct. The fact is, some of the issues we struggle with may be the result of our poor personal choices or habits to which the spiritual discipline of self-control needs to be applied. In these instances, we must learn to take personal responsibility and choose to partner with the Lord in changing these patterns.

It is also true that sometimes God allows the difficult situations in our lives to cause us to grow. In reading the story of Jonah, we discover that God used the plant to teach Jonah the kingdom principle that He loves all people despite what we may think or feel about them. It is important for us to recognize the seasons and situations that God is using to bring growth and maturity in our lives. In these times, standing against the enemy will not deliver us. Rather, submitting to the process and learning what God wants to teach us is crucial. If we don't, we will circle around the mountain again and again until we realize and accept what our heavenly Father wants to impart to us.

But when our issues become patterns in which sinful choices or thoughts have turned into strongholds that grip our minds, it is time for us to seek the Lord and to ask, "Holy Spirit, do I need freedom?" We need to seek divine help and guidance by welcoming in the Holy Spirit to this process by praying in essence, "Holy Spirit, help me in overcoming the battle in my mind."

Trust me. When we are genuinely inquiring, the Lord will be faithful to answer us and to lead us in a path of victory and abundant freedom.

LET'S PRAY FOR A TRANSFORMED MIND

Father, I thank You and rejoice in the truth that You are a good heavenly Father. I thank You that You created me as Your child and that I have a beautiful kingdom inheritance.

Holy Spirit, I invite You into the process of identifying and overcoming strongholds in my thoughts and my mind. As I begin this journey, help and guide me in identifying every area in which battles have been raging in my mind. Lord, I also welcome You to help me identify subtle thoughts and negative beliefs and emotions that keep me from walking out a victorious life in You. Show me every place in which I have embraced wrong beliefs. Reveal to me every place in which the enemy has spoken his deceits and lies.

Lord, I desire to walk with You, sold out, committed, and in a lifestyle of holiness. I thank You that this is a key strategic time in my personal relationship with You to be transformed from glory to glory. May I become a true reflection of You. I welcome Your truth, Your love, and Your delivering and healing touch now. Thank You, Lord. I am grateful and thankful for the opportunity to be whole and free. In Jesus's name, amen.

Chapter 2

DO I HAVE A STRONGHOLD
OF THE MIND?

*For the weapons of our warfare are not carnal, but mighty through
God to the pulling down of strongholds, casting down imaginations
and every high thing that exalts itself against the knowledge of God,
bringing every thought into captivity to the obedience of Christ.*

[2 CORINTHIANS 10:4–5, MEV]

A STRONGHOLD OF THE mind is based on a lie that Satan has established in our thinking—a statement we count as true but that is actually false. When we repeatedly listen to and entertain the lie, a stronghold is established. In 2 Corinthians 10:5 Paul describes strongholds of the mind as "arguments." The Greek word for "arguments" is *logismous*, which is also translated "imaginations" or "speculations." It also means things that we will believe and count as true. Below are some examples of strongholds of the mind:

- I know that I get too angry, but that's just how I am.

- I know that pornography is wrong, but at least I'm just watching the sexual sin and not actually sleeping with another person.

- I know that I should not think critically about other people, but I know more than others do.

- I know that being attracted to a man other than my husband is wrong, but I did not have sex with the man—I just kissed and touched him.

- I know that the Bible states that sexual attraction to the same sex is sin, but the world tells me that it's OK to be this way.

- I was born this way; therefore, I'm going to embrace the homosexual lifestyle.

- I know that things are really difficult in my marriage right now, but every marriage is difficult. These issues are just part of normal life.

- I want to be used by God, but I am not anointed enough. God really can't use me.

- I am not smart and can never succeed in school or in the job market. I always flunk tests and will never pass. I will never have a good paying job.

- Bad things always occur in my friendships. God does not want me happy or to have friends.

Lies such as those listed and any other lies we believe—whether they be about our physical selves, our personalities, our sinful behaviors, or our relationships with God or others—will act as a shield of confusion and entrapment in our thoughts to keep us from hearing the Lord. In time, a hardening of our hearts will occur, and we will have little or no ability to receive the loving conviction of the Lord in order to repent from our wrong beliefs and the resulting strongholds.

WE ARE TO LIVE BY THE SPIRIT

Before we continue learning how to identify strongholds in our minds, I want to briefly share with you a vital truth: *We are all called to live by the Spirit.* You see, God created us in

His image and likeness. The account in Genesis 2:7 clearly explains how the Lord formed Adam into three parts: "The LORD God formed a man from the dust of the ground and breathed into his nostrils the breath of life, and the man became a living being." Here we see that Adam had a physical body formed from the dust. The Spirit of God was made alive in Him when the Lord breathed His breath of life into Adam's body; this is the part of Adam that became His spirit man. Adam then became a living soul.

The soul is the part of our human nature that encompasses our mind, will, and emotions. As human beings, made in the image of God, we were created to live by the Spirit of God in us. Unfortunately, though Adam and Eve had been blameless before God, when they fell into temptation in the garden, sin entered into their lives and into the lives of every human born since then—except, of course, for Jesus.

How does this apply to you and me? All humans are made in three parts. We have our physical bodies, which is what the world sees when it looks at us. We have our spirit man, where the Lord dwells when we accept Christ as Savior. And we have our souls, which are comprised of our mind, will, and emotions. When we receive salvation, God breathes His Spirit—the Holy Spirit—into us, and our spirits become alive. We were created to then "walk in the Spirit," meaning we submit our bodies, minds, wills, and emotions to the Spirit of God, who is now alive in us. When we walk in the Spirit as our heavenly Father intended, we are empowered to experience spiritual victory in every aspect of our lives.

How do we submit to the Holy Spirit? We welcome His presence into our prayer lives and invite Him to be a part of our daily lives. He is available to us to guide, direct, and fill us with His overcoming love and presence. As we grow in a relationship with the Holy Spirit we discover that His presence becomes a divine source of peace and He becomes a close and cherished friend. His welcomed activity in our lives brings power, peace, love, truth, holy thoughts, and freedom.

First Thessalonians 5:23 further explains, "May the very God of peace sanctify you completely. And I pray to God that your whole spirit, soul, and body be preserved blameless unto the coming of our Lord Jesus Christ" (MEV). The Greek word that is translated as *completely* in this verse is *holothesis*. It means "whole through and through, complete to the end, undamaged, perfect." It is evident that Paul is saying our heavenly Father made it possible for us to come into a place in which our spirit, soul, and body can be found blameless. We must therefore welcome and allow the Lord to do a complete renewing work through our entire being—our body, soul, and spirit. Only when we walk in the Spirit will we be able to combat the enemy's strongholds in our lives.

One of our first steps in walking in the Spirit must be to turn from our old ways and our self to the new man or woman God is creating in us. The apostle Paul wrote:

> Strip yourselves of your former nature [put off and discard your old unrenewed self] which character-ized your previous manner of life and becomes corrupt through lusts and desires that spring from delusion; and be constantly renewed in the spirit of your mind [having a fresh mental and spiritual attitude], and put on the new nature (the regenerate self) created in God's image, [Godlike] in true righteousness and holiness.
> —EPHESIANS 4:22–24, AMP

In order for us to walk in personal victory over strong-holds, we have to lay down the old self, strip off the sin nature, and disarm the evil lusts, desires, and thoughts of the flesh. Then we must embrace the new nature of Christlikeness.

Even with a sin nature, we can gain victory over sin

patterns and ungodly thoughts, and walk in righteousness and holiness. I believe it is possible for us as Christians to reach a place of holiness in our lives whereby we can go a day or even two without sin. I am convinced that our desire for holiness can be made evident in our lives. And yes, I believe this can occur even in those hidden places in our thought lives that no one but God and we know about. As we seek the Lord and ask Him to keep us from temptation, the Holy Spirit works in and through us to aid us in this process.

When we are made alive in Christ and walking in the Spirit, we are equipped to recognize and to overcome strongholds that have become established in our lives.

WHERE DO STRONGHOLDS COME FROM?

Some of you might be asking, "How are strongholds of the mind established in the first place?" As you know, the enemy has never, nor will he ever, play fair. He can and does set up traps in our lives, much as he did in the life of Dan, whose story opens this book. Those traps, in turn, cause us to be in bondage to a stronghold in our thinking patterns. The traps that lead us into bondage can include trauma, betrayal, abuse, rejection, abandonment, accidents, bullying, ungodly control, angry family members, and so on.

A second avenue by which strongholds can be established is through what is termed a generational iniquity. Exodus 20:4–6 explains:

> No carved gods of any size, shape, or form of anything whatever, whether of things that fly or walk or swim. Don't bow down to them and don't serve them because *I* am GOD, your God, and I'm a most jealous God, punishing the children for any sins their parents pass on to them to the third, and yes, even to the fourth generation of those who hate me. But I'm

unswervingly loyal to the thousands who love me and
keep my commandments.

—THE MESSAGE

The actual Hebrew word used in this scripture for *sin* is
avown. It is translated "iniquity, guilt, a judicial state of being
liable for a wrong done." If past generations in our families
have worshipped idols, turned their backs on God, or hated
God, it has opened a door for strongholds to be passed down
our family line. The good news is that Jesus brought us forgiveness, grace, and mercy: "His mercy extends to those
who fear him, from generation to generation" (Luke 1:50).
Therefore, we can repent of the sin in our family line, be set
free from its demonic grip, and provide a righteous inheritance for ourselves and the generations to come.

My friend Anthony Turner shares his powerful testimony
of breaking free from such a stronghold:

> In 2011, while I served as senior pastor of Covenant of
> Faith, our church family often had the occasion to cele-
> brate some of our missionaries as they came home for a
> time of rest and recharging. My wife, Alicia, and I, along
> with the church family, did this each time by hosting a
> Global Missions Reception. At these family gatherings
> we had a potluck dinner and gave each of our returning
> missionaries an opportunity to share their experiences
> with the entire church family. The previous two years
> had been amazing ones for Alicia and me because we'd
> had the opportunity to take several international min-
> istry trips to Jordan, China, and Egypt. Part of the DNA
> of our church was a love for the nations, as we had mis-
> sionaries on almost every continent.
>
> It was also during this time that I was asked to
> serve on the board of several international ministries.
> One was Healing 2 The Nations International based
> in Mali, Africa. Despite all the nations I'd visited, I'd
> never been to any countries in Africa. This was not

a problem for me, because as much as I loved missions and the nations, I had no desire to go to any part of Africa. I felt that 90 percent of the people I knew who loved missions wanted to go to Africa. I would listen as people shared how the Lord had given them a love for Africa and how He'd stirred their hearts. Their excitement left me with an outward smile and a "Praise the Lord," but inwardly I expressed a sarcastic, "Whatever!" I could not explain why I felt this way, nor did I see anything wrong with it until one of our missionaries began to share about his most recent assignment in Benin, Africa.

As he spoke, he talked about one of the sites he had visited on the coast of Benin in the port city of Ouidah—which still has the holding cells from which Africans were sold by their own people into slavery. He gave a very detailed picture of the process that had taken place so many years before as Africans were ripped from their tribes, homes, and countries. While he expounded on his experience, I began to feel an indescribable stirring within me for which I had no explanation.

As our missionary elaborated on the process of the sale of slaves by rival conquering tribes, he told us that after the purchase and before the slaves were shackled and forced onto the ships, they were made to walk around the "tree of forgetfulness." Men had to go round it nine times, women and children seven. According to the stories and tradition, they were told that this experience would make them forget everything—their names, their family, and the life they had once had. They were made to renounce their homeland and vow never to return.

As our missionary continued speaking, the Holy Spirit began to reveal to my heart why there was this disdain within me for the very idea of going to Africa. You see, I am of African descent, and my past ancestors were brought from Africa to the United States as slaves. I quickly realized that I was dealing with a generational curse and a stronghold of the mind that was operating in my life regarding the continent of Africa. I began to repent and to renounce the effects of this curse on my life. I asked the Father to give me His heart for Africa—and almost immediately I began to feel the result of my prayer.

I have since been to Africa twice, and I am making plans to return again in the near future. Not only have I been set free from the curse pronounced upon the slaves, but I walk in a supernatural authority while on the continent of Africa. Since my first trip, I now realize that I have kingdom assignments and destiny in Africa that the generational curse was attempting to prevent. On my most recent trip in August of 2013, I experienced angelic reinforcement and the supernatural hand of God as I ministered His love. I am expectant of great things as I continue to pursue and follow the Lord's calling to this land and its people.

A third way strongholds can become established in our lives is by willful sin we choose to engage in. When we sin and continually fall prey to repeated sin patterns, we give the enemy access to our personal lives, our thought lives, and our emotions. In Ephesians 4:27 Paul instructs us to "leave no [such] room or foothold for the devil [give no opportunity to him]" (AMP).

The Greek word for *foothold* in this verse is *topos*. It is translated "place, location, region, room, opportunity." When we sin, we give the devil an opportunity to invade our lives as well as our thoughts, emotions, and areas of influence. Therefore, he establishes a grip of bondage. In order for us to have victory in these areas, we have to let go of old sinful patterns and embrace the new nature available to us through Christ. The key is that we must intentionally choose this pursuit of holiness, seek the Lord and His ways, and believe for awesome divine encounters with God that will bring transformation. My own testimony is an example of this process.

HOW WRONG CHOICES LED TO STRONGHOLDS IN MY LIFE

I was saved at a Baptist youth revival when I was twelve. I will always remember the night I was baptized. As the preacher lifted me up from the water, I felt a strong, wonderful sense of the Lord's peace, love, and acceptance envelop me. I did not know at the time what to call it, but I now know that it was the Holy Spirit resting on me. I was a new creature in Christ!

As I entered my teenage years, I read my Bible almost every night and had a deep desire to know the Lord and the Word of God. But like most teens, I faced peer pressure. My desire to be accepted by the popular crowd was intense. My thoughts continually drifted to the lies the enemy was speaking to me: "If you would just go to those parties and do what the popular kids are doing, you will be liked."

Slowly I found myself drawn into the party scene. Before long I was a regular party attendee. My first two years of college, in fact, were mostly spent attending all the hottest parties on campus. On the outside I was having fun, but on the inside I was miserable. I felt the conviction of the Lord almost constantly. But the lies I had believed had gained a foothold in my thoughts and had become a stronghold. I had chosen a lifestyle of rebellion, and by doing so I permitted all kinds of ungodly influences in my life.

I was blessed to have praying family and friends. Actually, one of my best friends, whom I will call Kathy, began to attend church and became very involved in the singles class there. She put my name on the prayer list, and every Sunday that singles group prayed that I would get my life right with the Lord. Soon I felt a powerful pull of the Lord in my heart. I began to cry out in repentance, even in the midst of my sinful lifestyle. Upon returning home from party after party, I lay in bed crying, asking the Lord for forgiveness, and then I'd read the Bible until I fell asleep. During this time, a powerful desire to meet a Christian man and to get married began to rise within me. Thank the Lord for praying parents, grandparents, and friends!

After several months Kathy convinced me to attend church. It felt good to be with Christians and to worship the Lord again. In a short amount of time, I began attending all the church services and the singles functions. The party scene slowly began to fade out of my life. I enjoyed my new friends. I particularly enjoyed getting to know one young man by the name of Greg, whom I started dating. But the enemy does not like to give up on us that easily.

I was still riding the fence between two lifestyles. Even as I grew more involved at church, I received phone calls from my party friends regularly. They would tell me how much they missed me and would invite me to the next party. I declined many times, but they were persistent. Finally, I accepted an invitation. I thought it would be a great idea for me to go and to share with them all the good things God was doing in my life. I just knew that Greg would want to go with me and help me explain to my friends the changes I was making. This way I would not have to face everyone alone. I had a plan.

I arrived at Greg's apartment confident that he would want to be a part of this righteous cause. I will say right here and now, God knows with whom to place us. When Greg opened the apartment door, I excitedly told him where I was going, and I invited him to come along. He listened quietly but responded abruptly, "I will not be a part of your rebellion. I will not go!" Then he slammed the door in my face! I am somewhat outspoken and feisty, and this made me mad. Now I would definitely go to the party to prove him wrong. He would see that I was no longer walking in rebellion. I knew that I would be able to go and withstand the temptation.

When I arrived at the party, it did not take long before the games of peer pressure began. I had decided that I would not drink that night, but my friends insisted. In an attempt to keep them silent, I held a glass of alcohol in my hand with no intention of partaking. This worked for a few minutes, but my friends proceeded to measure the top of my glass to ensure that I was drinking. They kept urging, "Come on, Becca. Take a drink!" In an attempt to regain control of the situation, I finally took a sip. As I did, something unexpected occurred. I quickly realized that the alcoholic beverage tasted *awful*. For the past two years, it had been my drink of choice, but now the taste was nauseating. It even smelled terrible. This got my attention. What was happening?

Perplexed, I set the glass down and sat down on the sofa. By this time, everyone was drunk and had forgotten about me. Suddenly all activity in the room grew still as I felt the Lord's presence beside me. I could not see Him, but I was aware that Jesus was standing next to me. It seemed to me as if the room began to move in slow motion. I sat reverently still as He started to point to every sin that was happening around me: "Becca, do you see that sin? That has been you for the past two years. Do you see that sin on the other side of the room? That has been you for the past two years." The Lord did this until every sin I had been involved in was pointed out. You see, friends, Jesus loved me so much that He came into that mess I had created in my life and expressed to me compassion, grace, mercy, love, and truth. Truthfully, He came to judge *for* me, not *against* me. I was broken and humbled, and I knew I must leave immediately.

Sobered by what had just transpired, I got up from that sofa, walked out of the apartment, and headed for my car. I was so overwhelmed by the reality of what I had become and the need to break out of this dark life that I said audibly, "Lord, I confess that I have been in blatant rebellion and sin. Please forgive me for all I have stood for over the past two years of my life. I say no right now to this lifestyle, and I will never return to it. It is over and finished."

From that moment I have never looked back. Nor have I had any desire to walk in that lifestyle again. That day it vanished from my life. Jesus was so good that nothing of that party world could ever satisfy my soul. As a believer, I had the power to choose a sinful life or a righteous life.

Because of the many wrong choices I had made during the previous two years, I had to go through a season of inner healing and deliverance. My rebellious and sinful choices had allowed demonic influences and ungodly thoughts and beliefs into my life that had to be dealt with and broken. I will share more of my testimony throughout the book. In the next chapter, I want to take a closer look at sin, but first, let's pray for God to give us a discerning heart as we examine what God calls sin.

LET'S PRAY FOR A DISCERNING HEART

Father, You know all things, and You know the intents and motives of my heart. You know every thought I think and how it took root in my heart. Lord, I pray that You open my eyes to see the sin I have allowed in my life that has led to strongholds. I pray that You reveal the wrong thinking that has put me in bondage, perhaps without my even realizing it. I pray that You reveal any generational sin or past trauma that may have contributing to wrong beliefs.

Holy Spirit, I know that You love me and that You want what is best for me. You have a good plan for my life, a plan to prosper me and not to harm me. I am willing to follow You and give up whatever is keeping me from walking in the fullness of victory over strongholds. Thank You for Your goodness and grace. Holy Spirit, open my eyes and ears as we proceed to learn about sin that can lead to strongholds. In Jesus's name, amen.

Chapter 3

RECOGNIZING SIN
FOR WHAT IT IS

I N ORDER TO live by the Spirit and thus be able to iden
tify and overcome strongholds in our lives, we have
to strengthen our spirit daily. To do that, we must be
intentional about growing in our spiritual walk. One key
ingredient in this process of growth is understanding what
the Word of God actually identifies as sin and then deter
mining to live free of these activities. One disturbing and
increasing reality I witness from those speaking in pul
pits is the unwillingness to call sin, sin. Sin is now being
called "bad choices" in an attempt not to offend those in
church services. As a result, more and more people are
totally unaware of what the Word of God considers sinful

Hear my heart—the gospel message is full of love and
grace, not full of legalism or condemnation. God is a God of
grace. As I shared in my personal testimony, I experienced
His amazing grace while attempting to live between two life
styles. But in that divine encounter with grace at that party,
Jesus was truthful in pointing out the sins I had committed
I experienced conviction of my sin, but not for one moment
did I feel condemned. Even in that grace-and-truth encounter
with God, I felt His unconditional love and holiness.

The truth is, grace produces the fruit of righteousness
John explains that Jesus, the living Word, came to bring
us God's grace: "The Word became flesh and made his
dwelling among us. We have seen his glory, the glory of the
One and Only, who came from the Father, full of grace and
truth" (John 1:14).

WHAT THE BIBLE CONSIDERS SIN

We must understand that failing to grasp the elementary truths of what is considered sin in the Word of God can create in us an open door to wrong beliefs and thought patterns. I fully believe that knowledge of the truth empowers us to think and act according to the nature of God and His kingdom, and to turn from the desires of sin, the world, and the flesh. For that reason, though the following list may seem elementary to some, I want to take the time to clearly indicate what God calls sin, and to present questions that allow for personal assessment. This will help you to identify whether a stronghold is in operation in your life. (Keep in mind that this is not an exhaustive list. We will further identify strongholds as we progress in the book.)

Committing adultery or participating in sexual immorality (Exod. 20:14)

Immoral sexual conduct, including adultery, thinking about having sex with someone who is not your spouse, pornography, bestiality, lust, prostitution, homosexuality, and so on, are sin and should be avoided (Lev. 20:10; Deut. 22:22; Matt. 5:27–32; 1 Cor. 6:13–20).

Questions for Personal Assessment

- Do you regularly think about sleeping with a person other than your spouse?

- Have you repeatedly struggled with addiction to pornography?

- When you are sexually intimate with your spouse, do you repeatedly imagine or think of another person?

- Do you believe it is OK to look at and think about sexual acts with someone other than your spouse?

- Do you find yourself frequently entertaining thoughts of fantasy lust (thoughts of sinful sexual practices that are not real but part of a fantasy life in the mind)?

- Have you frequented gentlemen's clubs or strip bars?

- Do you now have, or have you ever had, regular involvement with prostitutes?

- Are you struggling with thoughts of homosexuality or lesbianism?

- Do you ever think about engaging in sexual activity with animals?

- Do you view movies steeped in sexual perversion and find pleasure in doing so?

- Do you struggle with chronic masturbation?

- Even if you are married and faithful to your spouse, do your thoughts frequently drift to former sexual partners?

Covetousness (Exod. 20:17)

Coveting involves the desire or lust for things that are wrong or for what belongs to another person.

Questions for Personal Assessment

- Do you strive for as much wealth as possible because you feel that having money is the only way you will be valued or respected?

- When a friend gets a nice car or house, do you want to buy a nicer one?

- Do you feel anger toward those who have more than you do?

- Do you feel cheated when others have nicer things than you do?

- Do you believe that it is sinful to have nice things or that being poor is more spiritual than being rich? (This is a symptom of coveting as well as of a stronghold of poverty.)

- Does your mind constantly drift toward what the world has to offer rather than to what is holy and pure according to the Word of God?

- Do you easily conform to the world instead of setting a righteous Christian example?

- As a Christian, is your lifestyle different from that of your lost family members and friends?

Debauchery (2 Cor. 12:21)

Debauchery means following one's passions and desires to the point of having no shame or public decency.

Questions for Personal Assessment

- Do you find yourself dressing seductively in order to gain attention?

- Are you modest in your dress or purposefully provocative?

- Have you ever been asked by a supervisor to change your work attire to a more professional standard? (If so, this is an indicator that something needs to change.)

- Is the use of recreational drugs or the misuse of prescription drugs a problem in your life?

- Do you drink in excess or to the point of drunkenness? This is not to say that drinking in moderation is a sin, but does your drinking motivate others to drink too much? Do you feel as though you need prescription drugs, recreational drugs, or alcohol to alleviate stress in your life?

- Is flirting in public (in order to gain attention) a normal pattern for you?

- Do you become inappropriately loud in public places to draw attention to yourself? Do you need this attention to feel valued?

- Are you single and do you find yourself as one who has been and continues to be involved with multiple sexual partners?

- Do your thoughts frequently focus on sexual activity with different individuals?

Discord (1 Cor. 1:11; 3:3)

Discord is defined as quarreling, antagonism, and a struggle for superiority.

Questions for Personal Assessment

- Do you have thoughts or feelings of superiority, especially toward those in positions of leadership or authority?

- Do you gossip or share your opinions with others in order to gain a position of superiority?

- Do you repeatedly rehearse quarrelsome words in preparation to win future arguments?

- Some individuals like to "push others' buttons" because they enjoy quarrelling with and antagonizing others. Does this describe you?

- Do you frequently find yourself in arguments? Is quarreling and arguing a normal occurrence in your daily life?

- When in a heated discussion, are you able to choose righteousness and walk away from the situation, or do you purposefully continue to argue?

- Do you look to pick a quarrel or an argument with others?

- Are you resentful toward others and therefore make a point of arguing with people?

Dishonoring our mother and father (Exod. 20:12)

This commandment of the Lord regarding our parents includes all necessary acts of kindness, material support, respect, and obedience. Unfortunately, some parents are not loving or encouraging. Having been involved in deliverance ministry now for more than twenty-three years, I am very well aware of this sad truth. We will discuss the importance of forgiveness in chapter 5, but it is important to understand that even if one's parents don't "deserve" honor, the Bible instructs us to respect their position in our lives. This, of course, does not mean that we obey unlawful or immoral admonitions, nor are we to emulate ungodly behavior. But just as we respect the position of the president of our nation even when we don't agree with his decisions, we should respect our parents, even if they have not been good models for their children.

For those who have not had good parents, I believe God will be faithful to give spiritual mothers and fathers to honor. This might be a pastor, home group leader, Bible study leader, spiritual mentor, or a mentor in a chosen career path. Showing honor toward these individuals is a way to ensure that a lifestyle of dishonor is defeated.

Related to this directive of the Lord is the duty of the father and mother to love their children and to teach them the fear of the Lord and the ways of God. If you are a parent and you have not loved your children as the Word of God teaches us, now is the time to begin to do so. If abuse has been present in the past, get professional and spiritual help and stop this pattern. Repent to the Lord and ask your children to forgive you. Invite the Lord to bring healing to your life and your family. Perhaps abuse has not been an issue in your home, but there has been no spiritual growth occurring and you have not led your family in praying and reading the Bible. Make this the day of change and begin to experience the Lord, His goodness and love as a family. (See Deuteronomy 4:9, 6:6–7; Ephesians 6:4.)

Questions for Personal Assessment

- Do you have feelings of unforgiveness toward your mother or father?

- Do you hate your parents?

- Do you always have excuses when it comes to spending time with your mother or father? In other words, do you purposefully avoid spending time with them?

- Do you continually speak negatively or critically about your parents?

- Are you disrespectful to your mother or father, and if so, do you take pleasure in being so? As parents, have you been negligent in ensuring your children's salvation through Jesus Christ?

- Do you believe that it is not your place to guide your children to live a Christian life?

- Parents, do you enjoy demeaning and belittling your children, or speaking to them in a harsh manner?

- Do you pray together as a family?

- Do you teach your children from the Bible?

Dishonoring the Sabbath (Exod. 20:8–11)

In the Old Testament, the Sabbath was the seventh day of the week. To keep that day holy meant setting it apart from other days by ceasing one's labor in order to rest, serve God, and concentrate on things concerning eternity, spiritual life, and God's honor. In our day and time, we must be certain to make time for God each day in order to be filled with His presence.

Questions for Personal Assessment

- Do you consistently struggle to be committed to your daily prayer time and reading of the Word of God?

- Is your busy schedule more important than growing in your walk with the Lord?

- Do you avoid attending church or Bible studies on a consistent basis?

Dissensions (Rom. 16:17)

Dissensions are the result of divisive teachings not supported by God's Word.

Questions for Personal Assessment

- Do you think the teachings you have received are all correct, even if people have counseled you otherwise?

- Do you believe that the revelation you receive from God is somehow higher or more elite than the wisdom others have received?

- When wise and proven spiritual leaders offer you guidance and counsel, are you teachable, and do you have a heart to reevaluate your beliefs and opinions?

- Do you find your thoughts are consistently drawn to unscriptural teachings and beliefs? If so, is this a pattern in your family line?

Double-mindedness (James 1:8; 4:4, 8)

Double-mindedness means to be of two minds—wavering, doubting, uncertain, and divided in interest.

Questions for Personal Assessment

- When you are outside the church, do people often comment that you act totally different than you do when attending church?

- Is your mind and thought life continually in a state of confusion?

- Do you consistently fluctuate from being sold out to God one moment to being ready to walk away from the faith the next?

- Do you act one way when you are with Christian friends and totally different when away from them?

- Do you believe the lie that the way you act in public should be righteous and good but that how you behave behind closed doors is unimportant, even if your behavior is ungodly and inappropriate?

While the following questions may sound extreme, trust me, I have ministered to people who struggle from bondage to these lies:

- Do you believe that you are the Antichrist?

- Do you hear voices that convince you that you are someone other than yourself?

Drunkenness or addictions (Eph. 5:18; 1 Thess. 5:5–8)

Drunkenness is the impairing of one's mental or physical control by overindulging in alcoholic beverages. This can also be applied to the use of drugs that lead to addiction.

Questions for Personal Assessment

- Do drugs or alcohol have the ability to calm you more than do prayer, the presence of God, and the Word of God?

- Do you feel strong compulsions to drink (thinking, "I have to have that drink")?

- Do you find yourself using prescription or recreational drugs in a compulsive manner?

- Are you able to achieve mental or emotional peace without drugs or alcohol?

- Since marijuana is now legal in several states, do you think it is acceptable as a believer to engage in the use of this drug?

- Do drug or alcohol addictions run in your family? If so, have you been successful in avoiding this bondage, or do you find yourself succumbing to its pull?

- Do you believe that because your family members have suffered with addictions, the same fate awaits you, or do you have faith that God can and will keep you from this bondage?

- Are you a compulsive shopper or spender, unable to control your spending?

- Do you have an addiction to food?

- Do you struggle with a bondage to gambling?

- Are you addicted to any other practices?

Factions (1 Cor. 11:18)

Factions are defined as selfish groups or cliques that create division within a congregation or an assembly.

Questions for Personal Assessment

- Have you been involved in more than one church split? If so, do you typically find yourself in the group that is dissatisfied and therefore leaves?

- Are you able to stay committed to a group of believers or fellowship for an extended period of time, or do you always find fault with each group and leave?

- When a superior or supervisor has upset you, have you intentionally spoken to others about the situation to cause division and strife?

- Does your local prayer group turn your prayer times into gossip sessions?

- When there is discord between you and someone else, do you go to the other person in an attempt to resolve the issue before talking with others, or do you speak to others before approaching the individual to bring resolution?

- Does it bring you pleasure to speak about other people's character flaws in order to expose them?

- Is it easy for you to speak negatively about your spouse or ex-spouse to your children? Do you believe these actions will cause the people who hear you to like you more and your spouse or ex-spouse less? Is this your intent in speaking negatively?

Fits of rage (Col. 3:8)

Fits of rage are marked by explosive anger that flames into violent words or deeds.

Questions for Personal Assessment

- Do you yell, scream, or throw or break things to intimidate others so that you can get your way?

- Do you angrily threaten your spouse with divorce in order to keep the upper hand?

- Do you typically make threats and give ulti-matums when engaged in disagreements?

- Do you feel empowered when you make threats and speak ultimatums?

- Do anger and rage surface quickly when you are in a confrontational conversation?

- Do you strike others out of anger and rage?

- Do you push others when you are angry?

- Do you have uncontrolled anger where physical aggression is used toward someone else?

- When angry, do you say the most hurtful thing possible to harm the other person emotionally?

- Do you enjoy making others cry?

- Do you get angry with yourself and speak harsh words about yourself out loud?

- Do you find yourself feeling angry toward God on a consistent basis?

- Do you find yourself experiencing road rage when driving?

- During times of anger and rage, do you lose control and harm others? In these times do you take personal responsibility and apologize, or do you blame the other person for your actions?

Giving false testimony (Exod. 20:16)

We are not to make false statements about anyone's character or actions. We are to speak about all people in a fair and just manner. Sadly, I have ministered to many people who choose to make critical judgments toward others. This causes a great mental battle that they must overcome. Why is this? Because the open door of critical judgment toward others becomes a magnet that attracts critical and tormenting thoughts in the mind of the one being critical.

Questions for Personal Assessment

- Is it a normal occurrence for you to think or speak about others in a critical manner?

- Does it bring you pleasure and comfort to think and speak critically of others?

- Do you feel more valuable when you can find fault with someone else?

- Is it easy for you to share negative, critical things about other individuals?

- Do you gossip on a regular basis?

- When you are pulled into a conversation in which gossip is occurring, do you excuse yourself, or do you stay and entertain the discussion?

- When you are asked to hold something in confidence, do you share it with others anyway?

- Do you speak critically about others without going to the person one on one and trying to work out the issue in a scriptural manner? (See Matthew 18:14–17.)

- Have you spoken negatively about a leader or a person of influence to cause others to think negatively about that leader?

Greed (Luke 12:14)

The Greek word for *greed* is *pelonexia*. It represents the thirst for more that comes from a covetous, selfish motive. Money and material things are not evil in themselves. It is the selfish love of money that crosses into greed that is sin. Each of us should heed Jesus's warning and examine whether selfishness is present in our lives.

Questions for Personal Assessment

- When God blesses you, do you tend to keep His blessing all for yourself, or do you have a heart to use it to bless others?

- Do you want wealth in order to have more power than others?

- Do you think you are more loved and blessed by God because you have wealth and that those who earn less or have fewer material things are "less than" you?

- Do you use your wealth to intimidate others?

- Have you gained wealth in dishonest ways?

- Would you consider breaking the law to obtain more money, wealth, and power?

Hatred (Gal. 5:19–21)

Hatred is an intense, hostile emotion that oftentimes carries with it thoughts of vengeance or the intent to act against someone. It emanates from a place of extreme dislike or enmity.

Questions for Personal Assessment

- Is hatred toward people of other races and skin colors part of your thought process and belief system?

- Do you believe people of other nations and races are "less than" you?

- Due to traumas from your past, is hatred of men or women a normal emotional condition for you?

- Do you consistently speak out words of hatred? As we will discover in this book, there is power in our words. Speaking out hateful words will cause a stronghold of hatred to take root in our lives.

Jealousy or envy (Rom. 13:13; 1 Cor. 3:3)

Jealousy is to be resentful toward someone else or envious of another person's success. It drives a person to lash out at those who are being used strongly of the Lord or experiencing favor in their lives. A jealous person is easily threatened and is self-seeking and self-promoting.

Questions for Personal Assessment

- Are you able to rejoice in others' successes?

- Do you feel threatened when others achieve success?

- When God uses someone powerfully, are you able to rejoice, or do you feel overlooked and dishonored?

- Do you struggle with thoughts of dislike or hatred toward people because of their successes?

- Have you consistently asked yourself: "Why does everyone else receive blessings and favor, but I never do?"

- Do you look for opportunities to speak negatively about others because of their successes?

- Do you feel a need to promote yourself instead of trusting God to do so?

- Do you blame everyone else for your lack of success?

Lying (Col. 3:9-10)

Lying means to deceive and speak deliberate falsehoods. A stronghold of lying will also cause a person to be confused concerning his or her sexual identity.

Questions for Personal Assessment

- Do you tell lies or half-truths in order to manipulate or control others or to get what you want?

- Do you believe it is appropriate to lie and misrepresent yourself on job applications in order to get a job? Have you done this in the past?

- Do you exaggerate stories in order to cast yourself in a positive light?

- When you were growing up, did you repeatedly lie to your parents, teachers, and authority figures? Do you still do this today?

- When people with whom you have a relationship present to you areas in which you have believed or engaged in something that is wrong or inappropriate, do you lie about their observations, or do you quickly admit the wrong?

- Are you in bondage to the lie that you were born to be in a sexual relationship with the same sex?

Making idols and bowing down to them (Exod. 20:4–5)

The prohibition against the worship of other gods requires that we make no image of them, nor are we to make an image of the Lord God Himself and worship that image. We are invited to have a personal relationship with Christ through the gift of salvation, and by knowing the truth of God's Word, receiving the revelation of the person and work of Jesus, and being filled with the Holy Spirit.

Questions for Personal Assessment

- Have you prayed the prayer of salvation?

- Do you believe that praying to an image or an idol is your only way to receive forgiveness of sins and salvation?

While we understand that idolatry is worship of an image that is made by human hands, it can also come in the form of placing some thing or activity before our personal relationship with God. Allow me to pose a few more questions to further guide this time of personal assessment:

- Do you regularly neglect your personal time with the Lord to watch a certain television show?

- Do you spend more time on social media than in developing a relationship with the Lord and reading your Bible?

- Are sports or hobbies more important to you than attending a church service or a Bible study?

- Is the hobby you are involved in consuming a large amount of your time and taking you away from quality family time?

- Is reading the Bible a priority in your daily life or an afterthought following your other commitments?

Misusing the name of the Lord (Exod. 20:7)

The Hebrew word for misuse is *shaw*. It means falseness, worthlessness, that which has no result or use, or a negative reference to an entity, event, or state. We are not to misuse God's name by making a false promise by His name. God's name and nature are to be honored, respected, held sacred, and used only in a holy manner.

Questions for Personal Assessment

- Do you habitually swear and use the Lord's name in vain?

- Even as a Christian, do you speak half-truths in business dealings in order to get ahead?

- Do you think critically of the Lord or of the Word of God and speak out these criticisms on a regular basis?

- Is it difficult for you to talk about God and the Bible in a positive manner?

- If you are able to speak positively about our heavenly Father, do you hear thoughts in your head refuting, mocking, or doubting these truths while you are declaring them?

Murder (Exod. 20:13)

The act of willful murder is considered sin. The unauthorized, unlawful taking of a life is forbidden. In the New Testament murder is condemned along with hate, which promotes one to desire the death of another (1 John 3:15), and any other ungodly action or influence that causes the spiritual death of another (Matt. 5:21; 18:6).

Questions for Personal Assessment

- Do you find yourself thinking about committing acts of violence against another?

- Do you feel pleasure when you think about harming others in a violent manner?

- Do you have consistent thoughts of suicide?

- Do you regularly use words or phrases such as "I hate that person"?

- Do you hate yourself and often wish that you had never been born?

- When individuals who dress and act differently from you (people covered in tattoos or body piercings, people struggling with homosexuality) come to your church, do you shun them and treat them poorly so that they will not return? Or do you reach out to them in the love of Christ in order to see their lives changed? Our actions can either lead a person to new life in Christ or spiritual death.

Pride or rebellion (Prov. 16:18)

We are all familiar with the phrase "Pride comes before a fall." Not only does pride cause us to stumble and fall, it also causes us to try to maintain an ungodly, sinful control over our lives that removes the Lord from guiding and directing us. First Samuel 15:23 says, "Rebellion is like the sin of divination, and arrogance like the evil of idolatry." The root issue of pride is focusing too much on "I," making ourselves, our opinions, and our thoughts the idol or object of our worship. Pride holds no regard for spiritual account-ability, the truth of Scripture, or the heart of the Father.

Questions for Personal Assessment

- Do you think you are always right?

- When you are right, is it necessary for you to point that out and make others state that you are right?

- Are you defensive when others try to bring you correction or offer constructive sugges-tions on how you can improve?

- Are you argumentative on a regular basis?

- Are you stubborn to the point of being unteachable?

- Do you think everyone else is always wrong but that you have the answer to every problem?

- Is it difficult for you to admit your own faults?

- Do you sincerely apologize to others when you have wronged them? (If you never take the initiative to say you are sorry, this is an indi-cator that pride is at work.)

- Do you dominate conversations in order to keep the focus on yourself and what is impor-tant to you?

- Can you genuinely listen to others?

- Are you angry and determined to be heard and always to have the last word?

- Are you critical and judgmental, and do you enjoy voicing such thoughts?

- Do you believe that it is prideful for you to receive a genuine compliment? When God has worked through you in a supernatural way, do you use terms or phrases such as "God did it all, and I had nothing to do with it"? If so, you may be walking in the deception of false or excessive humility, which is the same thing as pride.

Selfish ambition (2 Cor. 12:20; Phil. 1:16–17)

Selfish ambition is defined as seeking power for personal and self-centered gain.

Questions for Personal Assessment

- Do you believe that getting close to influential people will cause you to be recognized and to receive promotion?

- Is your motive for relating to others self-seeking? In other words, are you seeking only what you can get out of the relationship?

- Do you have a heart to serve and bless others, or is your main concern to look out for yourself and have influence over others?

- Do you feel the need to dominate situations so you can be seen and heard?

- Do you love others with the heart of God, or do you build relationships only for the benefit they can bring you?

- Do you believe God promotes us in life or that promotion comes from man?

Stealing (Exod. 20:15)

This commandment prohibits the stealing of money or anything belonging to another. Cheating is also a form of stealing. Honesty should be an attribute in all of our dealings.

Questions for Personal Assessment

- Do you believe it is OK to take something that is not yours because "you deserve it"?

- Have you ever stolen from your workplace because you feel you have worked hard and are entitled to do so?

- Do you repeatedly cheat on tests or at work in order to make your life easier?

- Have you stolen from your church, family, or friends?

- Have you ever lied about your accomplishments in order to get ahead or to gain favor? Have you done this at the expense of someone else?

Unbelief (Heb. 3:19)

Unbelief disregards God's promise of faithfulness to those who serve Him sacrificially with a pure heart. Unbelief does not accept the promises of the Lord; it causes those held captive by its lies to question the goodness, power, and faithfulness of God's Word. It paralyzes faith. Those who are bound by unbelief do not believe God for the possible or the impossible. They struggle to accept the love of the Father and to believe prophetic words concerning their destinies. Their thoughts are full of pessimism; they continually repeat in their minds and with their words the risks of following God.

Questions for Personal Assessment

- Do you feel God does not love you as much as He loves others?

- Do you believe that nothing good ever happens for you?

- When you read the Bible, do you believe that God's promises are for everyone else but that somehow they always elude you?

- Do you find it difficult to step out in faith and take risks in God's kingdom when He directs you to do so?

- Do you believe that God loves you, or do you blame Him for the negative things that have occurred in your life?

- Is it difficult for you to have faith in the goodness and love of our heavenly Father?

- Is it difficult for you to read the Word of God?

- Do you repeatedly or consistently fall asleep when you read the Word of God?

- Is it difficult for you to stay awake in church or during worship services?

- Do you feel hindrances to understanding the Word of God and the truths of God?

Unforgiveness (Matt. 6:14–15)

We will discuss unforgiveness in great length in chapter 5 and provide an opportunity for personal assessment at the end of that chapter, but as we continue the current discussion, it is vital for us to recognize that any area of unforgiveness will halt the growth of our personal lives, thought lives, emotional lives, and spiritual lives. The Bible instructs us to forgive, because unforgiveness leads us to a place of a torment in our thought life.

Witchcraft (Rev. 9:21)

Witchcraft refers to the attraction and power of witches, black magic, or sorcery. It is the counterfeit of the true power of the Son of God and the Holy Spirit. It is a spirit and a practice that functions in blatant rebellion to God. Witchcraft is completely opposite to the purposes of the Lord. Common practices that involve a spirit of witchcraft or divination are tarot cards, psychic readings, reading or writing horoscopes, using a Ouija board, and engaging in astrology or necromancy. Even certain forms of martial arts and yoga fall into this category. (See Appendix.) Any participation in witchcraft practices will hinder our relationship with the Lord.

Not only do Satan and the world offer witchcraft practices and beliefs, but there is also something called Christian witchcraft. This is the practice of praying your will for another person instead of praying God's heart—or using your will to inflict your opinions and control over another in a sinful way.

Questions for Personal Assessment

- Do you believe it is OK to visit psychics?
- Are you engaged in the daily reading of your horoscope?
- Do you own a Ouija board?
- Do you practice yoga?
- Do you participate in forms of physical exercise such as martial arts, the roots of which are steeped in paganism and bowing to the universal chi?

- Have you had regular participation in tarot card readings, séances, or Reiki?

- Have you participated in, or are you still involved in, forms of New Age spiritualism and meditation?

- Do you watch movies or read books steeped in witchcraft?

- Do you consistently pray your will for other people?

- As a Christian, do you wish evil or speak and pray curses toward those who are involved in witchcraft?

- As a Christian, do you regularly speak against other believers or manipulate others emotionally in order to get your way?

Worshipping other gods (Exod. 20:3)

As believers, our worship is to be directed to God alone. We are not to worship, pray to, or seek guidance or help from any other gods, beliefs, spirits, or the dead. We are not to worship spirits through spiritism or divination or any form of idolatry. We as believers should be totally consecrated to God. We are to seek and love God with all our heart, soul, and strength.

Questions for Personal Assessment

- Are you actively involved in spiritual practices separate from Christianity?

- Do you embrace Eastern religions along with Christianity?

- As a Christian, do you still participate in cultural traditions of praying to, worshipping, or appeasing dead ancestors?

- Do you visit or have you visited psychics, mediums, or those practicing witchcraft in order to gain direction for your life?

- Are you involved in Freemasonry, the Order of the Eastern Star, or any other type of fraternal organization whose foundations are established in pagan beliefs? (See Appendix.)

I want to state right now that "there is now no condemnation for those who are in Christ Jesus" (Rom. 8:1). Our God is a God of mercy, one whose mercies endure forever. If as you read through the list above and answered the questions for personal assessment you identified an area of sin and a resulting stronghold in your life, do not allow condemnation to take hold. The good news is that God's amazing grace, love, and truth set us free! If you need mercy, run to the all-merciful one. He will be faithful to forgive you and heal you.

A Prayer of Repentance and Renunciation

Father, I rejoice in the fact that Your truth sets me free. I welcome Your delivering anointing to envelop me now. Holy Spirit, guide me in this time of prayer, and highlight to me those areas in which I need to repent. [Allow the Holy Spirit to reveal to you every sin, sinful thought pattern, and stronghold that has gripped your mind. Do not rush this process. When you are ready, engage in a time of confession and repentance.]

I confess that I (or my past generations) have been involved in the sin of _____
in my thought life [specifically name the sins that have invaded your thoughts] *and I have embraced the lies of the stronghold of* _____
[specifically name the strongholds that you are battling in your mind].

Thank You, Lord, that in You we have redemption and through Your blood the forgiveness of sins. Thank You that Your blood is greater and more powerful than any of my mistakes and sins. You have come to rescue me from the enemy's hand. Jesus, I bring these issues to You, and I repent of them now. I ask that You forgive me for them.

I renounce, break, and cancel all activity of the stronghold of _____ [specifically name the stronghold]. *I speak to this stronghold and say that your hold on my thought life and actions are cancelled, in the name of Jesus. I am no longer submitted to your lies.*

I ask, Holy Spirit, that as my thoughts have been washed clean by Jesus's blood, You will fill my mind to overflowing with life, love, patience, freedom, joy, purity, goodness, holiness, humility, righteousness, and acceptance as Your child. I rejoice in Your glorious freedom! In Jesus's name, amen.

Chapter 4

HOW THOUGHTS AFFECT OUR EMOTIONS

*Those who live according to the flesh have their minds set on what the
flesh desires; but those who live in accordance with the Spirit have
their minds set on what the Spirit desires. The mind governed by the
flesh is death, but the mind governed by the Spirit is life and peace.*

[ROMANS 8:5–6]

GOD WANTS US to walk in abundant life and peace. As we discovered in chapter 2, the soul was designed to walk in submission to the Word of God by the power of the Spirit of God in us. Therefore, if our minds have been gripped by Satan's lies or wrong and sinful thinking patterns, not only will it affect the choices we make but also our emotional states. Tormenting lies and thoughts can and will become strongholds, which can create feelings of fear, anxiousness, worry, depression, confusion, and rejection.

This is what happened to Sarah. She was a beautiful teenage girl, but boys at school teased her and called her hurtful nicknames that they thought were funny. She repeatedly and kindly asked them to stop, but without fail the teasing continued.

After several months Sarah began to struggle with feelings of confusion, rejection, and depression. The lies of the enemy grew increasingly louder in her mind: "You are not as pretty as the other girls. If you were, those boys would not pick on you. You are ugly, fat, and worthless." Her parents could see that Sarah was shutting down emotionally.

She came home from school sad and withdrawn. Sarah's parents also noticed that her appetite had changed significantly, and she was not eating enough. Sarah began to lose weight, and every time her parents encouraged her to eat, she grew more and more defensive.

After much prayer Sarah's parents approached Sarah to try to figure out what was occurring so they could help their daughter. Sarah was so discouraged that she decided to open up about her situation. As Sarah shared her experiences with them, her parents realized that thoughts of rejection had so overcome Sarah that she was completely depressed. This depression, in turn, had caused her to enter into the beginning stages of bulimia. Sarah's parents prayed for their daughter, but they did not see any change in her.

The following weekend they brought her to a Christian gathering, where the minister was preaching about how to obtain freedom from wrong thinking patterns and negative emotions. Sarah's parents were elated that night as their daughter chose to make her way to the altar for ministry.

After receiving a word of knowledge, one of the ministers asked Sarah if she was being teased by boys at school. Sarah began to weep and quietly said, "Yes."

The minister then gently asked, "Sweetheart, are you struggling with bulimia because of this? Has the enemy spoken lies to you that you are fat and ugly?"

Again Sarah softly responded, "Yes."

"Would you like us to pray and see these thoughts stopped and your emotions healed?" the minister asked her. Cautiously, Sarah agreed.

That ministry time was precious and powerful. The minister stood in the gap and repented to Sarah for how she had been treated. He explained to her that the Lord did not want her to be treated this way, and prayed with her to address the stronghold of rejection and the lies it had spoken to her mind. She wept as she began to experience freedom. The minister then began to declare to Sarah the truth of her identity in Christ. "Sarah," he said, "you are a beautiful young woman. God makes no mistakes. He loves you." The minister and his wife then led Sarah in declaring: "I am beautiful. I have a beautiful body. God loves me. I am special. I am fearfully and wonderfully made. I am not sad, but I am happy and full of the joy of the Lord!"

As Sarah repeated the words out loud, she began to smile and laugh. Joy flooded her thoughts and emotions, and the strongholds that had developed in her mind and emotions were broken. Sarah has not struggled with bulimia since that encounter.

THINKING WITH OUR HEARTS

It is so wonderful to hear testimonies of freedom and victory over strongholds. I wanted to share Sarah's story because it shows how our thoughts can affect our emotions and how our emotions can affect our thoughts.

We have already quoted this verse, but I want to do so again: "As [a man] thinks in his heart, so is he" (Prov. 23:7, AMP). What does it mean to think in our hearts? The Hebrew word for *think* in this verse is *shaar*. It means "to reason out, calculate, reckon, and estimate." Can the heart actually reason? We think of the heart as an organ that facilitates the circulation of blood throughout the body. But scientific research has found that it also aids us in reasoning:

> In the 1960's and 1970's researchers John and Beatrice Lacey were first to discover that the heart "was not just a pump but also an organ of great intelligence, with its own nervous system, decision making powers and connections to the brain. They found that the heart actually 'talks' with the brain, communicating with it in ways that affect how we perceive and react to the world. Over

two decades of research, the Lacey's also found that the heart had its own logic, which often diverged from the commands of the autonomic nervous system."

In 1991, Dr. J. Andrew Armour introduced the concept of a functioning "heart brain," and showed that the heart has its own language and its own mind. In his book, *Neurocardiology*, coedited with Dr. Jeffrey L. Nardell, Armour reveals that the heart, as a "little brain," has an elaborate circuitry that allows it to act independently of the cranial brain—to learn, remember, even sense and feel. Armour demonstrated that "with each beat the heart sends complex signals to our brain and other organs. These heart signals are capable of reaching higher brain centers, ultimately affecting our reasons and choices, our emotions and perceptions."[1]

Some of us might be surprised to learn that our heart has an ability to reason. But I feel pretty certain that although we might not have known the scientific research, we already make decisions based on what our heart is sensing and speaking to us. This is why we are instructed to make Christ the center of our hearts. The apostle Paul writes:

> For this reason I bow my knees to the Father of our Lord Jesus Christ, from whom the whole family in heaven and earth is named, that He would give you, according to the riches of His glory, power to be strengthened by His Spirit in the inner man, and that Christ may dwell in your hearts through faith; that you, being rooted and grounded in love, may be able to comprehend with all saints what is the breadth and length and depth and height, and to know the love of Christ which surpasses knowledge; that you may be filled with all the fullness of God.
>
> Now to Him who is able to do exceedingly abundantly beyond all that we ask or imagine, according to the power that works in us, to Him be the glory in the

> church and in Christ Jesus throughout all generations,
> forever and ever. Amen.
> —EPHESIANS 3:14–21, MEV

The first part of Paul's request is that God, according to the standard of His glorious riches, might empower us to be strong so we can overcome resistance. To do this, God imparts living power into our inner being through the Holy Spirit. This inner being is our *eso*, or our soul (mind, will, and emotions) and our conscience. When our innermost being is thus empowered by the Holy Spirit then, through faith, Christ is able to dwell in our "hearts," which refers to the whole of our personalities.

The "dwell" discussed in Ephesians 3:17 refers not to Christ coming into our hearts at the moment of salvation. Instead, it signifies Christ's desire to literally "be at home in" our lives, that is, to be at the very center of, or deeply rooted in, our lives. God has divinely ordained that from this deep-rooted place we will encounter to the greatest supernatural extent the deep things of God. In so doing, Christ becomes the dominating influence in our attitudes, thoughts, emotions, and conduct.

It is difficult in our human thinking for us to fully comprehend the incredible, unending greatness of our heavenly Father. However, the promise God has given us is that in our innermost being we can receive more and more of His never-ending love, glorious presence, supernatural power, and awesome truth that transform our thoughts and our very being into His likeness.

This, of course, is not what the enemy wants. He doesn't want us to walk in the confidence of who we are in Christ. He doesn't want us to believe we are the beloved sons and daughters of God and the beneficiaries of His kingdom promises. To keep us from experiencing the fullness of the Father's love and recognizing our identity in Christ, Satan seeks to get us to think and react in emotionally negative ways. He wants us to worry, become depressed, and think no one cares—even our heavenly Father. Persistent negative emotions distort our thinking, thus creating strongholds that cause our emotions to function contrary to the will of God. Let's identify some of the most common ways strongholds manifest in our emotions.

Rejection

Rejection is by far one of the most common strongholds I encounter as I minister to others. Almost everyone has experienced rejection in one way or another. It can occur any time from conception to adulthood. When a stronghold of rejection is in operation in a person's life, that person ends up being rejected on a repeated basis. Making a person fearful of being rejected is exactly what this stronghold was assigned to do. Oftentimes individuals who suffer from rejection build what I term "walls of protection" around their heart and emotions. These walls, built to protect, ultimately hinder close, personal, meaningful relationships. So rather than protecting themselves, their behavior tends to hasten the sad and discouraging outcome they so fear.

There are many causes of rejection. Rejection can come from a belief pattern or a spiritual condition that has been passed down a person's family line, causing an individual to expect to be rejected. It can come from a violent conception, a woman's disappointment about being with child, or the manner of a child's birth. It can happen when a person is emotionally, verbally, sexually, or physically abused. Other ways a stronghold of rejection can take root in a person's life include having insensitive parents; being bullied by classmates; having unfair, negative, and critical teachers; being adopted; parents divorcing; a mother not bonding with her child after birth; or a betrayal. Rejection can also be based on wrong perceptions, thought patterns, and attitudes. The list is obviously quite extensive.

Rejection is a serious and, unfortunately, common issue in the body of Christ. But God is faithfully setting people free. John is just one example. I asked him to share his story in his own words.

> One Sunday as Becca ministered at her home church in Colorado Springs, she taught on deliverance from strongholds. She invited people to come to the altar for ministry so the Lord could heal them from traumatic experiences that had led to strongholds. I responded to the altar invitation because I felt that with the dysfunctional upbringing I'd had and all the traumatic experiences I had experienced both in my childhood and my adult life, there must be something that could be uncovered—and there was.
>
> I had struggled with the fear of rejection for a very long time. It was so strong that I felt that nobody could ever help me with this, including God. And I believed that nobody, including God, would want to help me. Throughout my adult life, even as a believer, I had learned to live with this stronghold and to get by in life. I had the knowledge that I was hidden in Christ, and I knew how to take certain thoughts captive, but I still struggled with these feelings in all areas of my life every day.
>
> Leading up to that Sunday, God had used a very difficult experience at my job, messages from my pastor, and a book that one of my corporate managers had given me to "prepare the ground." While I was at the altar that day, hoping that God would see my obedience, God showed me that a recurring dream I have had about my father was the reason I struggled with a fear of rejection. You see, my father died from a heroin overdose when I was ten years old. He never

rejected me; in fact, he always tried to make me feel that I was his best friend. However, whenever I had this dream about him, he was very distant and did not want to be in my life.

As Becca prayed and asked the Lord to show all of us any areas in which a stronghold was rooted in our lives, God showed me that my father's death had affected me as a form of rejection. Not only did a healing take place from a very deep emotional wound, but the Lord also showed me what the reoccurring dreams were trying to tell me, and He delivered me from that weighty chain of dysfunction on that Sunday.

He has started a new work in me. I am now living with a new authority over the fear of rejection. I am no longer consumed with the need to feel accepted, and I do not have false imaginations in my mind of what others are thinking about me.

I praise the Lord for what God did in John's life that Sunday. Sadly, I see so many people who suffer from the effects of a stronghold of rejection without understanding the cause of their suffering. In their book *Evicting Demonic Intruders*, authors Noel and Phyl Gibson describe the fruit of rejection:

> The roots of rejection produce three different fruit-bearing branches. Firstly, rejected people show a variety of aggressive attitudes. Secondly, they suffer from symptoms of self-rejection which may or may not be seen. Thirdly, motivated by their fear of rejection, they make constant attempts to avoid being rejected.[2]

Like John, many people suffering from rejection learn how to "get by" in life. But freedom is possible. Consider the following questions to assess whether a spirit of rejection has taken root in your life:

- Do friends consistently leave or distance themselves from you?

- Are you repeatedly battling thoughts that no one likes or cares about you? Do you voice these negative thoughts out loud?

- Are you aggressive in conversations or interactions with others in order to dominate and so protect yourself from being rejected?

- Are you passive-aggressive when faced with conflict? Do you seem to receive constructive feedback only to later respond aggressively behind the person's back, attacking the individual verbally?

- Do you believe you are worthless?

- Do you contend with low self-esteem or insecurities?

- Have you voiced out loud that you hate yourself?

- Did your parents divorce? As a result, do you suffer from thoughts of rejection and fear of abandonment?

- Do you believe the lie that if you had been a better son or daughter, your family would have stayed together? That is to say, do you believe that it was your fault that your parents divorced?

- Were you adopted and feel rejected and abandoned by your birth parents?

- Do you starve yourself or overeat because of feelings of rejection?

- Do you overspend because of emotional wounds and feelings of rejection?

- When others reach out to you as friends, do you immediately have to fight fearful thoughts that something negative will happen in the relationship?

- Are you excessively aggressive and defensive when people don't treat you the way you think you should be treated?

- Are you suspicious that people are always out to get you?

- Do you rehearse old wounds of rejection and have a hard time letting go of them?

- Is it difficult for you to forgive those who have mistreated you and move beyond that hurtful situation?

- Do you see God as a loving Father or as a taskmaster?

- Do you believe you must earn God's love and approval, or are you confident that He loves you unconditionally?

- Do you find yourself living in a manner that is restricted by rules to gain the approval and acceptance of our heavenly Father? Or does His love, presence, and Word guide your daily walk?

- Do you frequently think God is not pleased with you?

- Do you regularly have thoughts of guilt, shame, and condemnation?

Many of us know people who struggle with a pattern of rejection in their lives. It seems that these individuals always find themselves in hurtful situations that lead to the exact outcome they so desperately want to avoid. Or maybe you identify with this in your own life. The great news is that our God is an awesome, delivering God who makes available to you His healing love and power that can defeat all schemes the enemy uses against us!

Depression

Depression and anxiety are becoming a common problem in our nation and throughout the world. According to the Anxiety and Depression Association of America, anxiety disorders are the most common mental illness in the United States, affecting 40 million adults (18 percent of the US population).[3] At any point in time 3 percent to 5 percent of people suffer from major depression; the lifetime risk is about 17 percent.[4]

Anxiety disorders cost the United States more than $42 billion a year, almost one-third of the country's $148 billion mental health bill.[5] Studies go on to say that most people who struggle with anxiety also struggle with depression, or vice versa. I can honestly say that in our ministry we are praying for an increasing number of people of all ages who struggle with strongholds of depression or anxiety. A person who battles depression might exhibit a number of symptoms. Consider the following list of depression symptoms to see if this stronghold may be affecting you or someone close to you:

- Persistent sad, anxious, or "empty" mood

- Grief

- Crying

- Self-pity

- Shame

- Feelings of hopelessness, pessimism

- Feelings of guilt, worthlessness, helplessness

- Loss of interest or pleasure in hobbies and activities you once enjoyed

- Decreased energy, fatigue, being "slowed down"

- Difficulty concentrating, remembering, or making decisions

- Insomnia, early-morning awakening, or oversleeping

- Appetite and/or weight loss or overeating and weight gain

- Thoughts of death or suicide; suicide attempts

- Restlessness, irritability

- Persistent physical symptoms that do not respond to treatment, such as headaches, digestive disorders, and chronic pain

- Tormenting thoughts

- Confusion

- Cutting or bringing physical harm to one's body in order to distract from emotional pain

As a minister, it grieves my heart to see so many in the world and in the body of Christ who struggle with this stronghold. Scripture says that those who mourn in Zion are appointed to exchange a spirit of heaviness for a garment of praise (Isa. 61:3). God has not designed us to walk in a state of despair, anxiety, depression, or silent hopelessness but in joy, praise, and victory!

Fear and anxiety

As discussed previously, anxiety is a growing problem. I personally know many people who are currently on anti-anxiety medications. Why is this becoming such an issue in our day and time? Obviously, we live in a society in which there is increasing daily stress. We see disturbing turmoil in the world around us. It seems that as a whole culturally, we are pulling away from biblical values and principles. Sadly, the more we take God, His love, and His kingdom principles out of our culture, the more anxious and hopeless we become. He is the only true source of joy, peace, and comfort. No amount of human ingenuity or creativity can fill the void left when God is absent.

Many people today live very stressful lifestyles with great responsibilities. There are single parents raising their children and holding down one or more jobs to make ends meet. Even in two-parent households, increasing pressures are coming from our jobs, after-school activities, and other endeavors that leave us always feeling rushed and hurried. All of these can and do lead to worry.

What is worry? Our English word *worry* comes from an Anglo-Saxon word that means "to strangle."[6] I think we can all agree that worry certainly does strangle people physically, emotionally, and spiritually. The Bible term *merimnao*, which is often translated "be careful" or "to be anxious," means literally "to be torn apart." Worry comes when the thoughts in our minds and the feelings in our hearts pull in different directions and tear us apart. The mind thinks about problems, and negative feelings weigh down the heart, creating a vicious cycle that wrecks our emotional state. Our minds tell us we should not fret, but we often cannot control the anxiety in our hearts! If we want to enjoy peace, however, we have to break this cycle of worry.

And let's be really real. The forms of entertainment and physical activity that many participate in are steeped in witchcraft and violence. We will discuss this further in chapter 7, but I want to emphasize in this discussion that certain forms of entertainment (those steeped in violence, witchcraft, sexual perversion, vampirism, and the like) are an open door for a stronghold of fear, anxiety, depression, anger, confusion, and violence.

How does a stronghold of fear and anxiety manifest? The following list is not exhaustive, but it will give you a clear picture of how this stronghold could be paralyzing your spiritual growth and faith:

- Phobias

- Fear of death

- Panic attacks

- Fear of crowds

- Claustrophobia

- Fear of heights

- Fear of the dark

- Fear of authority figures

- Migraine headaches

- Accusations

- Confusion

- Depression

- Lack of trust

- Judgmentalism

- Nightmares and night terrors
- Stress
- Worry
- Timidity
- Torment
- Insomnia
- Suspicion
- Symptoms of schizophrenia
- Sorrow
- Self-rejection
- Unbelief

Often those who are bound by fear become people pleasers. They have a difficult time saying no and establishing personal boundaries, and they therefore end up living a life based on what others want for them instead of living out God's kingdom plan for their lives. This can lead to stress, depression, anxiety, and hopelessness. This fear and anxiety literally become a mental, emotional, and spiritual prison for the person. But the Word of God speaks clearly concerning the true victory our heavenly Father has provided for us:

> For [the Spirit which] you have now received [is] not a spirit of slavery to put you once more in bondage to fear, but you have received the Spirit of adoption [the Spirit producing sonship] in [the bliss of] which we cry, Abba (Father)! Father!
> —ROMANS 8:15, AMP

> God did not give us a spirit of timidity (of cowardice, of craven and cringing and fawning fear), but [He has

given us a spirit] of power and of love and of calm and
well-balanced mind and discipline and self-control.
                                    —2 TIMOTHY 1:7, AMP

No matter how busy and stressful the world around us
may be, we do not have to be slaves to fear and anxiety. We
can be free.

An orphan mind-set

God never intended for us to walk through life alone, yet
sadly, many people feel emotionally and relationally isolated.
This is exactly what the enemy wants. If he can get people to
believe his lies, thus causing them to be gripped by strongholds, often they will withdraw from relationships and life.
Without loving fellowship, a person is vulnerable to the enemy's efforts to wreak havoc on his thoughts and pull him
into even deeper bondage.

This withdrawal can be rooted in thoughts of shame, guilt,
condemnation, or fear (fear of rejection, fear of abandonment,
etc.). Another root cause can be what is commonly referred to
as an orphan mind-set. This is a mind-set that makes it difficult for a person to relate to God as a loving Father. Or it can
cause a person to feel great distance from God's love and the
love of others. Those who are plagued by this mind-set feel
that they are victims, always taken advantage of; therefore,
they avoid relationships. Usually those with an orphan mind-
set have experienced fatherlessness or motherlessness, or love
was not expressed freely in their home. Abuse or neglect also
may have been present in their upbringing.

I know people who literally will not leave their homes due
to an overwhelming fear of relating to others and the percep-
tion that all relationships will end in an emotionally negative
manner. Others will not leave because they have come into
such a deep place of depression that they have begun to give
up on life. Not only do these individuals suffer from great

loneliness, but hopelessness takes hold of them as well and leaves them no strength to press forward in life. If they are married, often their marriage begins to suffer because of the emotional distance created by this mind-set. Their friendships and family relationships often become superficial.

God understands the need for human companionship and the bond of Christian friendship. The Word of God says He "sets the lonely in families" (Ps. 68:6). Do you suffer from an orphan or victim mind-set and therefore experience loneliness? The following questions will help you in the process of evaluation:

- Do you go for days without leaving your home and relating to others?

- The longer you withdraw into your home, does it become more difficult for you to venture out?

- Does the enemy place lies in your mind such as, "The only safe place for you to be is in your home. It's a dangerous world out there"?

- Do you battle feelings of hopelessness (also known as hope deferred) and believe God does not want to help you?

- Do you find yourself staying in your home and not bathing or changing clothes for days?

- Do you fear building relationships because you might be disappointed?

- Do you go for days without any social interaction with others?

- Do you have regular thoughts that others will harm or disappoint you, so it is not worth it to build friendships?

- Do you suffer from thoughts such as, "I am always the victim; everyone takes advantage of me"?

- Are you able to relate to others but only at a superficial level because you feel ashamed or hesitant to share your true feelings?

- Do you think of God as a distant taskmaster who shows no love?

- Do those closest to you often say, "I have known you for years, but I really do not know you. You have walls up, and you never share truthfully about yourself."?

- Have you made the following statement or do you have the following thought frequently: "I will never let anyone get close enough to me to hurt me. This is the only way I can protect myself."?

If you can relate to any of these questions, take heart. You can be free indeed. This isn't a permanent state of being; this is the fruit of a stronghold that can be broken by the power of the Holy Spirit.

Anger

Anger stirs up strife, contention, heated discussion, and disagreement. It can cause a person to have thoughts and emotions of vengeance, and it brings about great harm through abusive words and violent actions. Proverbs 29:11 says, "A [self-confident] fool utters all his anger, but a wise man holds it back and stills it" (AMP).

As we discuss the realities of anger allow me to share a portion of my testimony. It begins with a prayer I prayed twenty years ago in a time of Spirit-led self-examination:

Lord, forgive me for the sin of anger. In every place in which I have stubbornly and emotionally determined to have the final word in an argument, I confess this as sin and ask Your forgiveness. For every time I have acted out of vengeance, I ask You, Lord, to forgive me. Holy Spirit, help me to overcome this sin of anger. I welcome You and give You permission to speak to me and to correct me before I open my mouth to lash out with hurtful words. I desire true change and abundant freedom. Help me to overcome this sin.

The Holy Spirit then spoke to me and led me in taking authority over this stronghold. I prayed out loud as He directed, "I say that I will no longer submit to emotional anger or entertain angry lies in my thoughts. Anger, I break your hold on my emotions, thoughts, and words, and I invite the peace of the Lord to reign in my life."

Having already experienced the faithfulness of the Lord to empower me in freedom and victory several times, I knew that He would help me. However, I did not realize the intense battle that I would face in walking out my commitment to not succumb to anger. In truth, there was a strong need for personal responsibility on my part in order for me to completely overcome this anger. I had to choose to believe and stand on the truth of God's Word, and to intentionally decide to deal with the wrong patterns and behaviors I had embraced. It was not long before my first test came.

My husband and I were young in our marriage and both headstrong and confident in our opinions. As in many marriages, often our strongly voiced opinions caused a clash of wills between my husband and me. One day Greg and I were in a heated argument. I will never forget the direction of the Lord to me in His faithfulness to keep His promise to deliver me: "Becca, do not open your mouth and say those words to Greg. Remember, you invited Me to correct you and to help you overcome the sin and stronghold of anger."

Upon hearing the Lord's correction, I stood in dead silence while fighting an intense internal emotional battle to keep my mouth shut. I quickly realized that the longer I stayed in my husband's presence, the harder it was for me not to yell at him. I have to admit that despite previously repenting and renouncing anger, I still wanted so badly to have the final angry word in this confrontation.

In obedience to the Lord's voice, I deliberately turned and walked to the room that would provide me the quickest escape from the emotionally charged situation. It happened to be the laundry room. I swiftly entered and shut the door behind me. Resting both hands on the washer and dryer, I began to pray out loud: "I speak to my emotions, and I say, 'Come into alignment with the Word of God. You will come into a place of peace. I will not lash out in anger at my husband. I will not say hurtful words.' Holy Spirit, come and bring peace to my emotions."

Now friends, this battle was so intense that I was physically shaking. Forget turning on the washer and dryer—my shaking and trembling in this spiritual battle caused both appliances to gyrate beneath my hands! But with the help of the Lord, after several minutes I got my emotions under control.

Following this incident, I had several other opportunities to control my anger that helped me break this cycle. With the guidance of the Holy Spirit and my choice to take personal responsibility to walk out my freedom from anger, I overcame the patterns and habits anger had produced in my life. I am pleased to report that I am no longer plagued by this spirit. And believe me when I say that my husband was genuinely thrilled when this spiritual victory was realized in my life!

How about you? Do you struggle with anger as I so obviously did?

- Do you find yourself losing emotional control in disagreements?

- Do you struggle with rage?

- Do you have thoughts of fear that push you to anger?

- Is the fruit of self-control absent in your life?

- Have others repeatedly spoken to you about your anger issues?

- Was anger a problem in your family line?

If you answered any of the previous questions positively, keep reading, because we will discuss how you can break this pattern in your life.

Confusion

Being under the influence of confusion is like walking through a thick fog. Confusion hinders our ability to see where we have come from or where we are going, and while we're in the fog, we see no clear way out of it. Confusing thoughts and emotions can be stirred up by a number of factors. They can be caused by disobedience to God, unrighteous living, traumatic circumstances, or living a life based on the fear of man instead of the fear of God. Oftentimes the enemy uses confusion to bring disunity and discord in key relationships in our lives. Its scheme is to get us totally off track from the Lord's plans and purposes.

One of the primary ways confusion enters is when we become more concerned about what others think than what the Lord has told us. When God has given us specific direction about something and we fear the opinions of others on the matter, we honor others more than we honor what God has asked us to do. Hear what I am saying. I totally believe that God is a God of honor—within our ministry we teach the concept of honoring and preferring others as better than ourselves. And there are definite protocols for us to follow in honoring other people if we want to move from one season to another with God's blessing and favor. What I am talking about here is an unholy fear of man that keeps us paralyzed from moving into God's best for our lives.

The reality is, it is not normal for Christians to be in a confused state. So what might a stronghold of confusion look like?

- When God calls you to serve Him, are you more concerned about what others will say than about being obedient to Him?

- Do you choose to stay in an ungodly relationship because you are afraid of hurting the other person's feelings when ending it?

- Do you have a difficult time committing to a marriage relationship? Allow me to explain this point further. Often people get an idea in their minds of what a "perfect" marriage partner is to be. They will go from relationship to relationship and if they find a character flaw or area in which a person needs to mature, they will refuse to enter that relationship—all because this individual does not reflect the spotless image they envisioned. I

have ministered to many lonely people who
are so bound by a stronghold of confusion
that they could not possibly commit to marriage until they are set free.

- Is there a history in your life of repeated
  broken relationships? Do you find yourself
  in a cycle of important relationships ending
  through discord and disunity?

- When in relationships and friendships, do you
  find yourself feeling confused and unable to
  commit to these people?

The Bible teaches us that our "God is not a God of confusion but of peace" (1 Cor. 14:33, NAS) and that He is "the
Light of the world" (John 8:12, NAS). If God is the light and
the truth, then how can there be confusion in our lives if
we are rooted and grounded in Him? Friends, live a life
founded on Him and in obedience to Him.

DAVID GOT IT!

So what do we do when these strongholds take hold of us
and so negatively impact our emotions? As I read the Book
of Psalms, I realized that David found victory over his emotions when he practiced bringing his thoughts, his soul, and
his emotions in line with God's goodness and truth.

Can you imagine what it must have been like for David?
He had been anointed by Samuel to become king. As a young,
valiant teenage warrior, he slew Goliath and delivered the
children of Israel from the threat of the Philistines. He
received incredible favor from King Saul and was made his
armor bearer and was welcomed into the royal family. But
Saul's favor soon turned to jealousy and double-mindedness.

David became the king's enemy. He spent many years

running from the very leader who had earlier extended his hand of favor and blessing to him. When the opportunity presented itself twice, David refused both times to touch God's anointed and kill Saul. All the while Saul broke his word not to harm David, and he continued to pursue David in order to kill him. I think we would all agree that this would be enough to cause many to fall into fear, unbelief, confusion, and depression. David's restraint not to kill Saul had to come from a deep place of trust in God.

In the Book of Psalms, we see David pressing beyond his circumstances, his thoughts, and the resulting depression into a place of victory. He cries out: "Why, my soul, are you downcast? Why so disturbed within me? Put your hope in God, for I will yet praise him, my Savior and my God" (Ps. 42:5). Here David is taking authority over his downcast emotions. I especially like the way *The Message* Bible expresses it this way: "Why are you down in the dumps, dear soul? Why are you crying the blues? Fix my eyes on God—soon I'll be praising again. He puts a smile on my face. He's my God."

In modern vernacular I think that David was saying something along these lines: "Soul, come on, why are you so sad? You shouldn't be so emotionally disturbed and confused. I'm choosing to put my hope in God. I will praise Him, because He is my Savior and my God, and He will never fail me!"

In Psalm 42:5 we see David in the kind of mental and emotional battle many of us face daily. Maybe we are not running for our lives, but we all face the battle of having to rise above what our negative emotions and thoughts attempt to dictate to us. The beauty of our personal walk with the Lord is that He has breathed His breath of life and His Father's heart of love into our spirit. We are filled with His love, goodness, and authority. Realizing this, David spoke to his soul and directed it to hope in God. Then he chose to praise the Lord, which as we will discover is so very key in overcoming warfare in our minds and souls.

LET'S STOP, PRAY, AND PRAISE

Jesus, thank You for the price You paid on the cross. How grateful I am that You carried the weight of the sins of the world. I thank You that through the cross I have been blessed with forgiveness and redemption of sin. And I thank You that You have made a way for my emotional healing and wholeness.

Lord, I repent for walking in [specifically name the emotional issue you are struggling with]. *I choose this day to serve You. I confess that by Your stripes I am healed. I declare that I am no longer downcast, confused, fearful, depressed, rejected, lonely, or angry. I declare that I am not an orphan or a victim. I cancel every stronghold that has gripped my emotions and thoughts now, in Jesus's name.*

I receive Your love, peace, comfort, joy, and acceptance. Lord, flood me with Your Father's heart of love that I may know with great confidence that I am Your child. I welcome personal encounters with Your loving-kindness and goodness.

Give me the grace to walk in self-control. I receive a garment of praise. I speak out loud that I am walking in a spirit of adoption by which I cry out Abba, Father. I have power, love, and a sound mind. Lord, I thank You that I am fearfully and wonderfully made and that You make no mistakes. I know that You have a prophetic purpose and destiny for my life.

I rejoice in Your goodness. I exalt Your name. I place my hope and trust in You. In Jesus's name I pray, amen.

Chapter 5

FINDING FREEDOM
THROUGH FORGIVENESS

*While He was yet speaking, a crowd came. And he who
was called Judas, one of the twelve, was leading them. He
drew near to Jesus to kiss Him. But Jesus said to him,
"Judas, do you betray the Son of Man with a kiss?"*

[LUKE 22:47–48, MEV]

MOST PEOPLE HAVE experienced betrayal, hurt, and wounding. These are never pleasant to endure, especially when they are caused by someone close to us. Such experiences do position us, however, to share in the sufferings of Christ, and they present us with an opportunity to become more like Him.

Can you imagine what those painful final days of earthly ministry must have been like for Jesus? After three wonderful years of healings, deliverances, supernatural encounters, raising the dead, teaching, and performing numerous signs and wonders, Jesus experienced one wounding after another when circumstances tragically turned against Him.

There were the religious leaders who were jealous of Jesus's popularity and threatened by His power and authority. To put it bluntly, they hated Him. There was Judas, the sadly deceived disciple who thought the payment of thirty pieces of silver was worth betraying his Master. I can't imagine what it must have been like for Jesus to be betrayed by someone who had walked with Him for three years. Jesus and the twelve disciples had experienced incredible kingdom moments together, lived life together, and ministered together.

After Judas there was Pilate, the spineless governor of the Roman province of Judea, who tried to wash his hands of any responsibility for Jesus's suffering and death. Then there was Herod, the powerless Jewish king to whom Pilate sent Jesus in order to get a second opinion about what was to be done with Him. Herod mocked our Lord. The chief priests and teachers of the law who watched the unfolding drama ridiculed Him as well. And we cannot forget the crowd that shouted, "Crucify Him! Crucify Him!" Do you wonder, as I do, how many in that angry, death-seeking crowd had witnessed our Savior heal the sick, cast out demons, and raise the dead?

There was Barabbas, the renowned criminal who gained his freedom at Jesus's expense. And what about those in the Roman army who mercilessly beat our Savior beyond the point of recognition? Then there were Peter's three prophesied denials, which came to pass just when Jesus needed His closest friends the most. Finally, the Roman soldiers nailed the Lord to the cross, cast lots for His clothes, and mocked Him, saying, "If You are the King of the Jews, save Yourself" (Luke 23:37, MEV).

As Jesus hung on that cross, He carried the weight of the sin of every person who has walked the earth, including you and me. Yet after His persecution, the numerous betrayals, the excruciating physical beatings, and the unimaginable agony of His crucifixion, Jesus became the ultimate example of forgiveness. While facing the very ones who were torturing Him, Jesus cried out from the cross, "Father, forgive them; for they know not what they do" (Luke 23:34, KJV). It was a demonstration of mercy unlike any that had been witnessed in that day and time, and a powerful example to us.

THE IMPORTANCE OF A FORGIVING HEART

Even as I write about the pain our Savior endured, what Jesus went through is hard for me to fathom. Let's be honest. With the extreme persecution and injustice that Jesus suffered, He certainly could have blamed others and cried out, "Why Me? This is unfair!" No one has had a better excuse. But instead, Jesus asked our heavenly Father to forgive His persecutors. He provided a way for those who had so mistreated Him to receive the benefits of salvation that His sacrifice on the cross promised to all who would believe—a life of joy, peace, forgiveness, freedom from all strongholds, and a personal relationship with God. In His response to His persecutors, Jesus modeled for us how to truly refuse anger, bitterness, and unforgiveness. He even taught us how to pray for our enemies and to bless those who persecute us.

You see, when we choose to genuinely forgive those who have hurt us, it makes a way for us to ask our heavenly Father to forgive us. In Matthew 6:14–15 Jesus says, "If you forgive other people when they sin against you, your heavenly Father will also forgive you. But if you do not forgive others their sins, your Father will not forgive your sins." When we confess our sins to God but do not forgive others, we are asking God to do something for us that we ourselves are not willing to do for others.

As we discuss forgiveness, there are two issues I want to quickly address. Often when individuals suffer through difficult and traumatic situations, they become angry with God. They blame Him for their pain, and they bring His goodness into question: "How could God allow this to happen? Why didn't He protect me?" The Bible teaches that we live in a fallen world. People sometimes make horrible decisions, especially those who have not received salvation. God is grieved when bad things happen to His children and when His children make tragic and harmful mistakes. Our heavenly Father is a loving God—His love is more immense than we can comprehend. It is important for us to realize that the bad things that occur in our lives are not God's fault. He is not the one to blame.

The other issue I would like to address is our need to forgive ourselves. Each of us has been affected by mistakes we have made that have led to anguish and loss. Even though these events cannot be wiped out, we can learn from the poor choices we have made, and those lessons can result in great maturity and spiritual growth. The problem is that we sometimes beat ourselves up and resist being set free from thoughts and feelings of guilt. The truth is, when Jesus hung on the cross, He forgave us of our sins. Our trespasses have been washed away by His blood, and they are completely removed from us as far as the north is from the south and the east is from the west—in other words, they are gone forever! If Jesus has forgiven us our mistakes, we should do the same.

RECOGNIZING THE LIES

We may know that Jesus died for our sins and for the sins of all humankind and that He is a forgiving Savior, but the enemy wages an intense battle against us to keep us from living a lifestyle of giving and receiving forgiveness. This is because he knows unforgiveness and bitterness will keep us bound mentally, emotionally, and physically.

When we choose not to forgive, we allow a spirit of unforgiveness to influence our lives. This lying spirit will convince its victim that when we do not forgive, we are punishing the one who caused us pain. But it is the one withholding forgiveness who ends up trapped. The one bound by unforgiveness will be convinced that no one can be trusted, thus causing the individual to build emotional walls that inhibit close relationships. Unforgiving people always blame others and keep a running checklist of every hurtful word, action, and deed people have inflicted on them. In many cases, as stated previously, they blame God for their pain.

Unforgiveness and bitterness rejoice in vengeance. One of the most common lies of unforgiveness is, "The one who inflicted the hurt does not deserve forgiveness." In reality, that might be true. But Jesus did not take this position, despite the fact that every one of those who harmed Him truly did not deserve the mercy He afforded them.

The sad truth is that if we do not forgive those who have hurt us, then the traumatic event that wounded us in the first place will control us. We will not be freed by withholding forgiveness but rather enslaved. And in time, if we refuse to forgive, a spiritual wall much like a fortress will block our freedom to have a growing personal relationship with the Lord. To put it bluntly, all spiritual growth will cease, and our prayers will be hindered. Again and again, I have seen people who have harbored unforgiveness in their hearts for long periods suffer greatly from tormenting thoughts, mental confusion, shutdown emotions, hardness of heart, depression, physical sickness, and extreme anger.

No matter what has been done to us, whether it be small or large, the end result of unforgiveness is the same. When we choose not to forgive someone, bitterness, resentment, and anger take root inside us. These in turn begin to dangerously infect our emotions and thought lives—no matter how right we think we are and how wrong the other person may have been. It is true that the other person might have sinned against us and hurt us in a way we could have never hurt someone else. But that does not minimize nor stop the effect unforgiveness has inside us.

We can find ourselves making comparisons between ourselves and the other person, portraying ourselves as spiritually superior to that individual in an effort to justify our unwillingness to forgive. But attempting to claim we are better than the other person does not work, nor does it bring us any peace. Instead, the offense we suffered is added to, day by day, because of our own unforgiveness—until it finally consumes us, and the person we truly are is lost in a sea of resentment, which brings emotional, mental, and physical torment.

But the good news is that if you want to be free from the poison of unforgiveness, bitterness, and resentment, and the devastating consequences they bring to you personally, and to your family members, relationships, health, and security, you can choose to forgive now. You too can pray the prayer Jesus prayed: "Father, forgive them!" When you do, the chains of bondage that have gripped your thoughts and emotions will be broken, and you will begin your life of freedom.

TRANSFORMED BY FORGIVENESS

It was a particularly warm evening in Africa with no air conditioning in the building where the conference meetings were being held. I have to confess, I was not feeling favorable toward engaging in a long altar-ministry time due to the heat that night in the sanctuary. However, as I spoke during the meeting, the Lord clearly directed me to teach on the lies of a stronghold of rejection and the power of forgiveness to see this stronghold defeated. The Spirit of God moved mightily on people's hearts as many wept throughout the message.

Upon completing the teaching, I invited everyone who wanted freedom in their thoughts and emotions to make their way to the altar. As people were walking to the front, the Lord highlighted one young woman to me. She wore a hat pulled down over her forehead in an obvious attempt to avoid having to make eye contact with others. She continually looked down to the ground and was extremely soft-spoken. I laid hands on her and began to pray.

As I prayed, the Lord showed me that this woman had been abused repeatedly as a child. I gently asked her, "What is your name?" and in a whisper she responded, "Miriam." I then shared with her what the Lord showed me: "Miriam, I feel the Lord is showing me that as a little girl you were repeatedly abused. Is this true?" Shyly she nodded her head in agreement. Based on the message I had shared that night, she understood that unforgiveness would keep her bound by traumas from the past and block her emotional healing. Of course, I explained to her that forgiveness and trust are not the same thing—the Lord would not want her to entrust herself to someone who continually abused her or to put herself back in harm's way. But it was necessary for her to forgive so that she would no longer be bound by rejection, fear, depression, and torment in her mind and emotions.

Miriam willingly forgave the man who had brought such hurt and pain into her life. As she did, I prayed that the lies of these strongholds in her mind and emotions would be broken and that the love of the Lord would bring healing to her. She began to weep tears of joy as the Lord touched her powerfully.

I hugged Miriam and then made a request of her: "Miriam, you do not need to cover your beauty with this hat. You are a beautiful woman, and the Lord wants you to have good and healthy relationships. I don't want you to walk with your eyes always shamefully cast to the ground. You need to take this hat off and walk with your head held up and a smile on your face, rejoicing in the Lord and His love. You are a beautiful daughter of the King of kings, and He desires that you experience the fullness of His love, joy, peace, and acceptance. I would like to request that tomorrow when you attend this conference, you come to me without this hat on, and give me a big hug and a report on your spiritual and emotional condition." She smiled and agreed to do as I suggested.

The following morning, our ministry team was waiting for the elevator to go to the sanctuary for the first morning session. A strikingly beautiful young woman approached and stood waiting at the elevator beside us. She smiled at me, and I graciously smiled back. Then she spoke to me in a questioning voice: "You do not recognize me?" Trying to place her in my mind, I asked, "Have we met before?" She said gently, "I am Miriam." Thinking that I had misheard the name, I asked, "What is your name again?" She smiled a confident smile and said, "I am Miriam, the girl with the hat! You prayed for me last night. I am free!"

Friends, I was elated and startled all at the same time. I had never witnessed such a dramatic change so quickly in someone to whom I had ministered. This woman did not look at all like the same person. Everyone waiting for the elevator broke out in joyous laughter and weeping. I embraced Miriam and wept tears of joy with her. God had so miraculously set her free that within this twelve-hour period of time she was a completely transformed young woman. Forgiving her perpetrator had transformed Miriam's life immediately.

THE BENEFITS OF FORGIVING

As Christians, we forgive from a place of forgiveness. What do I mean by this? As born-again believers, the price Jesus paid on the cross to bring us forgiveness is a part of our kingdom identity. And once Jesus is alive in us and breathes His Spirit into us, the same ability He had to forgive is living in us and made available to us through Him. If we choose to step into the beautiful gift of forgiveness that is extended to us and active within us, God will give us the ability, or the grace, to forgive. Now is the time for us to hear and believe the Word of God, embrace the powerful prayer that Jesus prayed on the cross, and walk in obedience to His example. When we choose to pray this prayer of forgiveness:

- It transforms our relationship with God.
- It releases the power of the Holy Spirit in our lives.
- It brings us great peace and joy.

- It restores our mind and emotions.

- Tormenting thoughts and accusations no longer harass us.

- It often welcomes God's healing where there has been sickness.

- It transforms our personal lives.

- It transforms our relationships with other people.

- It releases the favor of God in our lives.

- It releases the Lord's blessings.

- The Word of God comes alive to us.

- Freedom in worship is restored.

- There is no longer a wall hindering our prayers, so we can seek the Lord with great joy and freedom.

- Our prayers are heard by the Lord.

- We see answers to prayers.

THE CHOICE IS YOURS

The Bible is full of promises of restoration and hope for the people of God. It is exhilarating to read the Word and see the rich inheritance God has given to each of us. He is an off-the-charts amazing Father. But He also attaches conditions to His promises, and one of those conditions is that we must make the choice to forgive.

We all have the rest of our lives to live. No matter what has happened up to this point in life to bring you hurt and pain, you can choose to forgive now. The pain of the past does not have to continue into your future. As you have read this chapter, maybe you realized areas of unforgiveness in your life. To ensure that there is no stone left unturned, take a few moments to consider the following questions:

- While reading this chapter, did anyone come to mind whom you have not forgiven?

- Have you said you forgave someone who hurt you, only to find that you were still angry when you came in contact with that person?

- When you think of a painful situation from the past, do your emotions still "sting"?

- Do you rejoice when bad or negative things happen to the person who hurt you?

- Do you have feelings of vengeance toward anyone or desire revenge for a past wound?

- Do you rehearse in your thoughts actions that will harm those who have hurt you?

- Do you speak out loud words of hatred toward people who have disappointed you?

- Do you find yourself repeating out loud the mistakes of your spouse or children to make them feel guilty or unworthy? Does this bring you pleasure?

- When your loved ones do not behave in a manner that you feel is right, do you begin to harbor feelings of anger or unforgiveness toward them? For example, if your spouse does or says something in the presence of others that you think is inappropriate, are you able to talk with him or her about it and work through it, or do you allow anger or resentment to build up? Another example: if your children behave inappropriately or in an embarrassing manner while they are growing and maturing, do you get angry and resentful toward them instead of teaching them how to behave in a wiser fashion?

- Are you angry with or do you blame God for the negative things you have seen and experienced?

- Are you resentful toward yourself for traumas you have experienced or sinful choices you made in the past?

- Are you able to not think on or discuss hurts from the past, or do you still find yourself dwelling on these memories? When these memories arise, are you able to dismiss them, or do feelings of hurt surface at their memory?

- Do you feel a wall blocking your spiritual walk with the Lord? If so, when did this begin? Did it begin around the same time a hurtful situation or conflict began?

- Do you have feelings of hatred toward countries or people groups that your nation has warred against?

- Do you find yourself disliking or being angry with certain people because your family has done so for years?

- Do you have unforgiving feelings toward ungodly governmental leaders?

- Are you bitter toward the church?

If you answered yes to any of these questions, this is a strong indicator that there are individuals or situations you have chosen not to forgive. Out of obedience to the Word of God and with the help of the Holy Spirit, will you right now make the choice to forgive? Some of you may be in agreement with this and realize your need to forgive, but you do not feel an overwhelming urge to release the ones who have hurt you. My counsel is that you walk in obedience to the Word of God and follow the example that Jesus modeled on the cross. Your emotions will eventually catch up with your choice to follow our Savior's lead. You have nothing to lose and absolutely everything to gain.

A Prayer of Forgiveness

Lord, thank You for Your truth and for Your amazing love. I am so grateful for the price You paid on the cross for me and for every person who has ever lived. Thank You for forgiving my sins and bringing the gift of salvation into my life. It is Your truth and love that set me free.

I desire to walk as You walked—in a lifestyle of forgiveness. I confess that I have not been willing to release and to forgive some who have betrayed and disappointed me. But now, today, I make the choice to forgive each person who has treated me poorly, betrayed me, made false accusations against me, brought dishonor into my life, abused me, bullied me, or lied to me. [Name any other action done to you that has caused unforgiveness.] *I choose to forgive* _____ [name out loud anyone whom the Lord is showing you to forgive], *and I ask that You forgive this person/these people.*

Lord, in every area of my life in which I have been angry with You, I ask that You forgive me. I choose to believe in Your goodness, truth, and love.

In every area of my life in which I have not forgiven myself, I choose right now to release myself. Lord, I know that You love me, and therefore I choose to love myself. I speak to you, unforgiveness and bitterness, and I say that in every place in which you have taken hold of my emotions, I cancel your hold now.

Father, Your Word tells us to bless those who persecute us, so now, Lord, I speak Your blessing to each person whom I have chosen to forgive. Lord, touch each one of them with Your Father's heart of love. Teach me to love with Your heart. Teach me how to emanate Your heart of mercy, grace, and forgiveness. In Jesus's name, amen.

Chapter 6

HEALING THE MIND FROM THE SCARS OF THE PAST

For I will restore health to you, and I will heal
your of your wounds, says the LORD.

[JEREMIAH 30:17]

EXPERIENCING TRAUMA CAN have a dramatic effect on our bodies and our minds. Interestingly enough, even if we are not present when a traumatic event unfolds, simply witnessing it on television can bring us distress. According to medical studies, when we perceive a threat, our bodies activate what is called the stress response. This response occurs in both our bodies and our brains, but the impact of the trauma on the mind is often the more disturbing of the two. Traumatic events can leave us feeling unsafe. They can disrupt our beliefs and assumptions about the world. Our sense of our ability to control life also may be shattered, causing us to question how much influence we have over our lives and choices.

Most of us will remember for years to come the tragic bombing during the Boston Marathon on April 15, 2013. I remember sitting in my living room watching the news reports tearfully and prayerfully. It was difficult enough to see the events through the lens of the media. I cannot imagine how traumatic it must have been for those who experienced it in person. The reality is, this type of disturbing event can leave us distrustful of others or cause us to question in general to what extent we should trust people in the world. It can hinder our ability to be intimate with others and impact our feelings of self-worth. Additionally, those who are blessed to survive a trauma often feel guilt and wonder why they were not harmed when others were less fortunate.

As we grow, change, and have wide-ranging experiences throughout our lives, our beliefs and assumptions typically evolve over time. When we experience trauma, those beliefs and assumptions that help us make sense of the world around us change almost instantly. It is common for people to experience intrusive thoughts, worry, difficulty sleeping, trouble focusing, bouts of crying, blame or self-judgment, and lack of satisfaction. The effects of trauma also can cause extreme emotional fluctuations, unhappiness, anxiety, loneliness, anger, and irritability.

Undergoing multiple traumas or repeatedly being exposed to life-threatening events can have a further impact on our minds. Parts of our brain can become sensitized, causing us to be on high alert and to perceive threats all around, leaving us jumpy and anxious. Other parts of our brain that are associated with memory can actually shrink, making it difficult for us to consolidate and form new memories.

THE ENEMY DOES NOT PLAY FAIR!

Even when we have no influence or control over a traumatic event that occurs in our lives, Satan sees our suffering as an open door to bring additional wounding in the form of tormenting thoughts. Please remember this: *Satan has never, nor will he ever, play fair!* He will take advantage of an unsettling experience to gain a foothold in our lives. It is in our times of pain and emotional distress that the enemy will fill us with thoughts of fear, confusion, anger, rejection, distrust, unbelief, victimization, and the like. Remember, the enemy can bring these thoughts to our minds, but a stronghold is established only if we get into a pattern of entertaining his lies. As these thoughts and attitudes take hold, we become bound by the tormenting event.

Webster's dictionary defines *trauma* as "an injury (as a wound) to living tissue caused by an extrinsic agent, a disordered psychic or behavioral state resulting from severe mental or emotional stress or physical injury, an emotional upset."[2] Such an event might include but not be limited to the following:

- Rape

- A violent attack

- A car wreck

- A traumatic accident resulting in an injury

- Experiencing rejection while still in the womb

- Having parents who were driven by rage and anger

- Excessive teasing by schoolchildren or family members

- Being picked on or beaten up by a childhood bully

- Having alcoholic parents

- Experiencing sexual abuse or molestation

- The death of a loved one

- A long-term period of unemployment

- Seeing pornographic material as a child

- Being violated or victimized by another person

- Desertion or divorce

- Unfair treatment by a teacher or authority figure

- Total disappointment or letdown by trusted individuals

But friends, I want you to really grasp what I am about to say. Despite the traps of the enemy, our God will always make a way for us to come out of the past—whether out of bad, wrong, or sinful choices that we have made ourselves or traumas that have been inflicted on us by others—and into His glorious plan of redemption. The price that Jesus paid on the cross, the power of His cleansing blood, and His resurrection life are more powerful than any demonic scheme the enemy can conjure up against us. The Lord is an awesome God who stands against any and all traps, schemes, or accusations of the enemy.

In Colossians 1:12–13 Paul explains the spiritual exchange that takes place at salvation and the position in Christ that has been afforded to us. He writes that the Father "has qualified [us] to share in the inheritance of his holy people in the kingdom of light. For he has rescued us from the dominion of darkness and brought us into the kingdom of the Son he loves." The language used in this passage does not depict a casual episode. Jesus, the mighty conqueror, snatched us out of one condition and positioned us in another. Our Lord delivered us from the tyrannical dominion of darkness and drew us to Himself.

This was a transference from a skewed, ignorant, dark oppression and dictatorship to a well-ordered sovereign kingdom. As believers, we are now part of the Father's kingdom as His sons and daughters. If we choose to partner with the Lord and His mighty delivering work, then our God, His love, and His Word are powerful, magnificent, beautiful, and complete in leading us into freedom.

PETER'S DENIALS AND JESUS'S FAITHFULNESS

When I study the Bible, I like to read about Peter. For some reason Peter just seems human to me, and his passion and humanness can teach us great lessons for our lives. In one situation we see Peter anointed and sold out in complete, radical abandonment to the Lord; then in another situation he is being rebuked by Jesus. He had faith to walk on the water and was privileged to witness Jesus with Moses and Elijah on the Mount of Transfiguration. However, Peter suffered from what I will call foot-in-mouth disease and often spoke before he thought. He was obviously an emotional, passionate man, as was evident when he cut off the ear of a Roman guard in the Garden of Gethsemane in an attempt to protect Jesus from being arrested.

To be honest, these character traits of Peter's endear him to me. What must it have been like for Peter and the disciples to witness their beloved Messiah and teacher being unjustly arrested that night? Confusing, frightening, and traumatic, I'm sure. For Peter, I believe, it was exceptionally traumatic.

We are all familiar with the story. Before His arrest in Gethsemane, Jesus predicted that Peter would deny Him three times before the rooster crowed. Peter passionately exclaimed, "Lord, far be it from me to deny You!" But when Jesus was arrested, we read that Peter was asked three times about his relationship with Jesus and the other disciples, and he adamantly denied any connection. Just as Jesus prophesied, immediately following Peter's third denial the rooster crowed.

Luke 22:62 records Peter's agony, saying he "went outside and wept bitterly" (MEV). The Greek word translated *bitterly* is *pikros*. It means "with agony or mental suffering." Peter, in his distressed emotional state at the events unfolding in Jesus's final hours, reverted to a place of human fear, confusion, and anxiety. He vehemently denied the Lord whom he had so passionately tried to defend moments earlier. Peter was learning that he was not as strong as he had believed he was, and that resulted in deep grief and mental suffering for him.

We know that, mercifully, this was not the end of the story! After Jesus died, He arose from the grave and began to supernaturally appear to His disciples. Jesus appeared to a group of them twice, but in those first two meetings the issue of Peter's three denials was not resolved between the Lord and Peter. In John 21 we read of the encounter that released Peter's healing.

Peter, Thomas, Nathanael, the sons of Zebedee, and two other disciples were together. Peter decided to go fishing, and the others accompanied him. I have heard many say that in making this decision, Peter was disheartened and wanting to give up on Christ's calling on his life. I would like to take the opportunity to view this scenario from another perspective.

As I read this account under a prophetic anointing, I came to believe that Peter was reminiscing about all the miraculous kingdom moments that he had experienced with Jesus at the Sea of Galilee. He probably longed for the life he and the other disciples had lived together with Jesus before the Lord's crucifixion. I realize that this is my belief, but I would imagine that Peter had been experiencing an internal battle in his mind and emotions since his three dreadful denials of the Lord. You see, it was at the Sea of Galilee that Jesus had fed the five thousand. Peter and Jesus had walked on the water of the Sea of Galilee. It was here that Peter had caught the fish with the coin in its mouth and here that Jesus had calmed the storm. I believe it was a special place to Peter, and he wanted to be where Jesus had performed these miracles that had greatly impacted his life.

Do we not do the same thing? After a loss or a traumatic event, do we not find our thoughts and memories returning to special places we had been before the event occurred? My father passed into heaven on January 21, 2008, and to this day I think on the times he and I fished together at my parents' pond. In fact, the last evening I spent on my parents' farm before my mother relocated, I stood on the bank where my father and I had fished together so many wonderful nights in order to feel connected to those beautiful moments again.

As Peter walked by the sea and launched out in his fishing boat with the other disciples, maybe he hoped Jesus would appear to him and the others again at the Sea of Galilee—and friends, that is exactly what happened.

Following the disciples' completely unsuccessful night of fishing, Jesus appeared on the shore. He shouted out to those in the boat, "Throw your net on the right side of the boat and you will find some [fish]" (John 21:6). When the disciples did as Jesus instructed, they caught a large number of fish. In fact, their net was so heavy they were unable to haul it into the boat. John, the beloved disciple, suddenly realized that the man on the shore was Jesus and exclaimed, "It is the Lord!" (John 21:7). When Peter heard this, in typical Peter fashion he immediately wrapped his outer garment around himself and jumped into the water in order to reach Jesus quickly. The others returned to land by boat. When they arrived, Jesus already had a campfire started with a supernatural provision of fish cooked for His friends.

When they had finished eating, Jesus directed His attention to Peter:

> Simon, son of John, do you love Me more than these [others do—with reasoning, intentional, spiritual devotion, as one loves the Father]? He said to Him, Yes, Lord, You know that I love You [that I have deep, instinctive, personal affection for You, as for a close friend]. He said to him, Feed My lambs.
>
> Again He said to him the second time, Simon, son of John, do you love Me [with reasoning, intentional,

spiritual devotion, as one loves the Father]? He said to
Him, Yes, Lord, You know that I love You [that I have
a deep, instinctive, personal affection for You, as for a
close friend]. He said to him, Shepherd (tend) My sheep.

He said to him the third time, Simon, son of John,
do you love Me [with a deep, instinctive, personal
affection for Me, as for a close friend]? Peter was
grieved (was saddened and hurt) that He should ask
him the third time, Do you love Me? And he said
to Him, Lord, You know everything; You know that
I love You [that I have a deep, instinctive, personal
affection for You, as for a close friend]. Jesus said to
him, Feed My sheep.

I assure you, most solemnly I tell you, when you
were young you girded yourself [put on your own belt
or girdle] and you walked about wherever you pleased
to go. But when you grow old you will stretch out your
hands, and someone else will put a girdle around you
and carry you where you do not wish to go.

He said this to indicate by what kind of death Peter
would glorify God. And after this, He said to him,
Follow Me!

—JOHN 21:15–19, AMP

I love the heart and actions of our Lord. He fed Peter
before He dealt with his sins. How like the Lord to bless
us first and then put His finger on an issue in our lives that
needs healing!

As Jesus dealt with Peter, He focused first on Peter's
love for and dedication to Him, and then He dealt with
the kingdom calling on the disciple's life. Because Peter's
denials were made audibly three times, the truth had to be
spoken out three times to cancel the negative effects. And
because Peter had denied Christ publicly, Jesus made a way
for him to make it right publicly.

You see, if we really love Christ, our lives will be completely devoted and dedicated to Him. This exchange between Peter and our Lord provided the way for Peter's obedience and dedication to the Lord to be secure. The wonderful part of this encounter is that Jesus gave Peter a new commission. I believe the Lord designed this entire encounter to reawaken Peter's conscience, bring healing to his emotions and his mind, reverse and break the power of the three audible denials, and open the disciple's eyes to his soon-to-unfold kingdom destiny. The fact that Peter was clearly forgiven by Jesus and given new responsibilities amounting to apostleship despite his total denial of his Lord can give genuine hope to those today who feel they have denied Jesus and done something unforgiveable.

Our Savior is loving. He seeks out moments for us to encounter Him in order to bring us into freedom and victory. Friends, when we have these moments with our Savior, nothing and no one can take away the glorious victory they bring. This is why I so appreciate this encounter between Jesus and Peter. Just as Jesus showed up for Peter to set him free, the Lord showed up for me in my rebellion.

Do you believe the Lord loves you enough to want to set you free from trauma and hurt? I *know* that He does. What He did for Peter, He will do for you. Jesus wants to meet us in our places of trauma, hurt, and disappointment and to release His unending, merciful, gracious, magnificent healing love to us. All that is required of us is that we humbly seek Him and His love, and He will come to meet us in our deepest need.

A SENSELESS TRAUMA

Mike was an exceptionally gifted dancer and artist. From a very young age, he was drawn to ballet and jazz dance. Unfortunately, the men in his family were all athletes and grew concerned about Mike's interest in the arts and dance.

They feared he would grow to embrace a homosexual lifestyle and were very outspoken about their intense disap-
proval of his dancing. Even so, his mother insisted that he
be allowed to dance.

When Mike reached the age of twelve, his uncle (the only
father figure in his life) decided it was his responsibility to
ensure that Mike would be sexually attracted to women and
not to men. Therefore, he arrived at Mike's home with a box
that he called a "special gift." He escorted Mike to the back
bedroom of the home and encouraged him to open the gift.
It was full of pornographic material. He stayed with Mike in
that room until he had viewed many of the magazines and
videos in the box.

Needless to say, Mike was greatly traumatized by this sad
event. His uncle had ridiculed him for his love of dance and
was now forcing him to view pornographic pictures and
videos. Unfortunately, this was not the end, as he returned the
next day to ensure that Mike had viewed everything in that
box. For years to come, Mike and his uncle ritually viewed
pornography together. Mike grew up feeling rejected, violated, disgusted by his uncle, hurt, and angry that his mother
did nothing to stop the perverse actions. As a result of his
uncle's actions, Mike developed a chronic, sinful addiction to
pornography, fantasy lust, and masturbation.

Thankfully for Mike, when he was nineteen years old a
friend invited him to church. Within a couple of months,
Mike received salvation. However, his addiction to pornography and fantasy lust remained a hidden sin and continued
to increase. After a period of time, Mike met a beautiful
Christian woman and fell in love. A year after they met,
they married. All the while Mike continued to keep his
deep-seated thoughts of rejection and sexual addictions
a secret. In his heart he prayed that once he married, he
would finally feel accepted, and his desire for pornography

would diminish. The sad reality was that the exact opposite occurred—his desire for and thoughts about pornography grew stronger, not weaker. Mike was in deep despair and felt he could never overcome this hidden sexual sin.

Six months into their marriage, Mike told his pastor about his bondage to pornography. After hearing of Mike's need, the pastor asked me if I would help him in ministering to Mike. He knew that there were strongholds that had gripped Mike's thought life and emotional desires, and he felt I would be able to help him in this area.

When the pastor and I met with him, Mike shared with us his distressing story. His thoughts were consistently flooded with the words of rejection his uncle had spoken to him and the pornographic pictures he had viewed that fatal evening when he was twelve. He had felt unprotected by his mother, who knew this was happening.

I asked Mike if he had forgiven his uncle for accusing him of being a homosexual and exposing him to pornography. He quietly thought and then shyly said, "No, I don't believe I have."

"Have you forgiven your mother, who knew what was happening?"

Holding back tears he responded, "No."

I then asked one more question: "Mike, have you forgiven yourself?"

His response was quick and sure: "No."

The pastor and I led Mike in a time of forgiving his uncle, his mother, and himself. We also led him in a prayer asking the Lord to forgive him for all the unforgiveness he had harbored and for the sins he himself had chosen to commit that had empowered the bondage of perversion. We prayed concerning the trauma that had gripped his emotions and the stronghold of perversion that had entrapped his thought life from his initial and continual exposure to pornography. We invited the presence and the love of God to embrace Mike. God's love was tangible, and Mike began to sob. We watched as the healing power of God erased the pain of the trauma from Mike's past. It was a beautiful and glorious encounter.

I asked him to repeat this prayer out loud: "In Jesus's name I speak to my thought life and emotions, and I tell you that I will no longer live a life bound by rejection, perverse thoughts, fantasy lust, and pornography. Your assignment in my life is canceled. I renounce you in my thought life and emotions. The stronghold of perversion and pornography is finished. Lord, I commit myself to You and Your Word, and I welcome holiness and purity to flood my thoughts and my emotions." It was a beautiful sight to watch as Mike began his process of freedom.

The pastor established an accountability partner for him. And Mike purchased software that would send a report of all the activity he had participated in on his computer every day to his accountability partner. Mike began to study the Bible on a regular basis and declared the truths written in the Word of God. He faithfully participated in weekly counseling sessions with his pastor. The rejection that had plagued him was no longer a part of Mike's identity, and the struggle with sexual addiction ended. He and Emily now have a beautiful marriage, and Mike's ministry to the body of Christ through dance is awesome.

The Healing Process

Maybe you have experienced trauma or made decisions in the past that have brought pain into your life. If this is you and you have never received healing or relief, I want to take the time to walk you through the healing process. As we go through the following steps, it is my prayer that God will begin to reveal to you any areas in your life that need His healing touch. Let's welcome the Holy Spirit to lead us in a few moments of examination:

> *Father, I thank You for the revelation that You can bring healing to any and all traumas. Lord, I desire to be free from all trauma. I say yes and amen to walking unhindered with You. I recognize that there are areas in my thoughts and emotions that need Your healing touch. Holy Spirit, I invite You to come and to show me these places. Lord, I welcome Your goodness, revelation, and victorious love to guide me now.*

Now, sit down in the Lord's presence and allow Him to speak to you. Make sure you have a pen and paper handy. If a traumatic event that you have experienced comes to your mind, write it on your piece of paper. Below are some questions to guide you in this process:

- What past trauma is the Lord bringing to your mind?

- Do you harbor thoughts of revenge, dislike, anger, hatred, or unforgiveness toward those involved in the traumas? (If so, make a list of these individuals whom you need to forgive. Then pray the prayer of forgiveness that you will find at the end of this chapter.)

- Do you believe God does not love you or that everyone is against you?

- Are you mad at yourself?

After you have allowed the Lord to reveal any past traumatic events and individuals you need to forgive, pray the following prayer:

Lord, thank You for revealing to me the unhealed areas in my life. God, I welcome Your love and Your presence to embrace me now. Everyone who has brought hurt, pain, and trauma into my life through events in my past I choose to forgive now in Jesus's name [speak out the names of all those you are to release and forgive].

For every time and way in which I have questioned Your goodness and love and have blamed You, I ask that You forgive me. For every wrong belief or lie that I have embraced in my thought life and emotions, I ask Your forgiveness. I choose now to release myself from any and all anger, guilt, shame, and condemnation that I have heaped on myself. Jesus, Your blood sets me free. You have made a way for me to walk victoriously. I know that You love me.

So now I choose to break the power of all trauma in my thoughts and emotions. I cancel in the name of Jesus any and all rejection, fears, anxiety, confusion, lack of trust, and addictions [insert here any other issues that need to be spoken out loud in this prayer] *that have kept me bound.*

Lord, I thank You that You fill me with Your Spirit and Your love. I am Your child. You love me. I receive now the freedom and love that You have made available to me. Father, I say yes and amen to the plans and purposes that You have for my life. I believe that I am fearfully and wonderfully made. Your Word says that I am the head and not the tail. I speak to my mind and emotions to be full of joy, peace, comfort, love, patience, and long-suffering. I know that I am accepted and loved by You, Lord. I thank You, Lord, for this freedom from the pain of

*the past and that I am no longer bound. I rejoice
in You and praise Your awesome, magnificent, and
holy name. Amen.*

Remember, friends, God does not bring condemnation. In closing this chapter, I want to encourage any of you who are struggling with sexual addictions, drug addictions, alcohol addictions, or any other form of addiction to go to your pastor, ministry leader, deliverance minister, or counselor. Do not allow any guilt, shame, or condemnation to bring torment into your thoughts and keep you from receiving the help you need. Allow yourself to walk through a healing process with those who are gifted to assist you through an accountability process. You do not have to live your life bound by the lies of the enemy. God can and will set you free. You can choose today to turn your life around and to walk in glorious freedom with our Lord.

Chapter 7

WATCH WHAT YOU ALLOW
INTO YOUR LIFE

Therefore the children of Israel cannot stand before their enemies. They
turn their backs to their enemies because they have become dedicated
for destruction. I will not be with you anymore if you do not destroy
the things dedicated for destruction in your midst. "Get up! Consecrate
the people and say, 'Consecrate yourselves for tomorrow, for thus says
the LORD, the God of Israel: "Things dedicated for destruction are in
your midst, O Israel. You are not able to stand before your enemies
until you remove the things dedicated for destruction from your midst."

[JOSHUA 7:12–13, MEV]

T HE WORD OF God teaches us that physical objects
can have spiritual connections. Just as bad thoughts,
emotions, and attitudes can affect us, as we have discussed through the first several chapters of this book, so
can the possessions in our homes have a negative spiritual and emotional impact on our lives. What do I mean
by this? If there are items in your home that focus on evil,
violence, witchcraft, idolatry, perversion, and other sinful
things, they will prove to be a red-carpet invitation to
demonic harassment and evil thought patterns and beliefs.

If we entertain violent video games, then our thoughts
become focused on violence and aggression. If we read or
view perverse books, movies, magazines, and websites, then
our thoughts will become flooded with perversion. If we
have souvenirs from our travels that represent pagan gods
and goddesses, these items can open a door for unbelief.
Maybe we have a box or a drawer full of old love letters and

cards from a past ungodly relationship, and thoughts of this former boyfriend have never left our mind. Or perhaps we have a cabinet full of old journals and diaries in which are written only negative thoughts of depression and rejection, and every time we read them, they stir up negative thoughts, beliefs, and emotions in us again.

Could it be that what we have in our homes and what we engage in for entertainment can have a negative impact on us mentally, spiritually, and emotionally? I believe that the answer is yes.

OUR POSSESSIONS REFLECT OUR PRIORITIES

Our possessions are a reflection of our priorities. They basically show our true spiritual condition. What we view on television, in movies, and online will influence our thoughts and emotions. Holding on to possessions from the past that stir negative memories is actually a sign that we really do not want to move on. Let me explain further.

There are always moments when our homes are not clean— and not just unclean but in complete disarray. The kids' rooms are a mess. The kitchen is cluttered from the previous meal. The laundry needs to be folded and is stacked high waiting for someone to take on the task. The trash needs to be emptied. And some of the furniture is so dusty that we could write our names on it! This is the moment when we do *not* want anyone to come over for a surprise visit—and this is probably just when the dreaded sound of the doorbell is heard throughout the house.

What if someone paid a surprise visit to every drawer in your home? Or a surprise visit to your cell phone or computer? What if the history of every movie and television show you have watched over the past month was made public? (I am not saying that watching television is bad; we just need to use wisdom in choosing what we watch.) Many people would not find this hypothetical scene intimidating because they do not engage in activities that would bring embarrassment. However, some might be thinking that a surprise visit like this would not be a good idea because of what someone would discover.

The scriptural truth is that God does not want us to have anything among our possessions that dishonors Him. The more we grow in our relationship with God and experience His purifying fire, the more we will want our possessions to reflect and honor Him. Such an attitude will become a natural outflow of our lives. In the Old Testament, when the Lord spoke to Gideon, He warned His people to tear down the altars of Baal, cut down the Asherah poles, destroy idols, dismantle pagan altars, and build an altar to Him:

> That night the Lord said to Gideon, Take your father's bull, the second bull seven years old, and pull down the altar of Baal that your father has and cut down the Asherah [symbol of the goddess Asherah] that is beside it; and build an altar to the Lord your God on top of this stronghold with stones laid in proper order. Then take the second bull and offer a burnt sacrifice with the wood of the Asherah which you shall cut down.
>
> —JUDGES 6:25–26, AMP

A New Testament example is found in the Book of Acts:

> Many of those who had practiced curious, magical arts collected their books and [throwing them, book after book, on the pile] burned them in the sight of everybody. When they counted the value of them, they found it amounted to 50,000 pieces of silver (about $9,300).
>
> —ACTS 19:19, AMP

What items should we avoid? Read the following for some suggestions.

- Demonic books

- Books steeped in witchcraft, vampirism, were-wolves, death, and violence

- Objects, gifts, jewelry, love letters, and other items from past sexual or ungodly relationships

- Souvenirs that portray demonic beings, idols, or pagan gods or goddesses

- Journals or notebooks full of writings that rehearse a depressed state or emotion

- Books and movies related to Harry Potter, Twilight, or witches

- Ouija boards

- Buddhist, Hindu, or other Eastern worship artifacts

- Art that depicts pagan beings and worship

- Art and posters with skulls, snakes, spirits depicting death, gargoyles, etc.

- Items related to Satanism, witchcraft, New Age meditation, yoga, the zodiac, crystal balls, tarot cards, etc.

- Hard-rock music and material with images of darkness

- Things related to horoscopes and geomancy

- Good luck charms, amulets, fetishes

- All things pertaining to secret societies such as Freemasonry, Order of the Eastern Star, Skull and Bones, DeMolay

- Masonic jewelry, aprons, books, etc.

- All jewelry, clothing, and objects attached to Eastern religion and demonic beliefs such as yin and yang or Egyptian demonic symbols

- New Age occult symbols

Objects of Torment

Jamie was raised in a Christian home, but she went through a season of rebellion. She was drawn into witchcraft and became a master Reiki instructor and healer, and a well-known practitioner of Wicca. Her parents were grieved by the choices she had made and prayed for more than five years for the Lord to touch her heart.

One night Jamie phoned her mother and exclaimed, "Mom, I need help. I need Jesus. I can no longer be involved in these witchcraft practices. Please help me."

Her parents brought her to church, and she received salvation, but Jamie continued to be mentally, spiritually, and emotionally tormented. They called our ministry for help. I met with Jamie along with several of our ministry team members. The Lord began to touch her life and set her free. But soon it was as if we hit a wall. Jamie was still greatly tormented at night, suffering mental confusion and extreme emotions.

We set a date for me and the team to visit her home. When we arrived, it soon became clear why Jamie continued to suffer. She still had her entire healing crystal collection, idols of Buddha, New Age and occult music that she had used in her Reiki massage and healing services, and many other items of a demonic nature. We explained to Jamie why these objects were not permissible if she was going to be a Christian. These items did not glorify God but rather darkness, evil, and sin.

Jamie quickly agreed that these items had to go. We threw some of them away that day. That night Jamie and her dad stood in her garage and proceeded to break all the New Age healing crystals and to burn the occult CDs. After this Jamie received incredible freedom. The tormenting dreams she had experienced at night stopped, the mental confusion lifted from her mind, and her emotional extremes disappeared. Jamie and her parents were elated and grateful for her newfound wholeness and freedom.

BREAKING UNHOLY TIES

Jamie's testimony is powerful. However, I realize that many people may not have delved into witchcraft as she did, so I will give another example that more people may be able to relate to.

Melissa was saved at the age of twelve. For several years she walked with the Lord, but in time peer pressure lured her into rebellion. She entered into sinful relationships and became sexually involved with several of the men she dated. The more she rebelled, the more miserable she became. After several years, she was in such despair that she returned to church. She repented and committed in her heart not to return to the life she had been living.

Soon she met a wonderful Christian man. Within a couple of years, they married. Following their wedding they were actively involved in their local church and began to be mentored for leadership. However, Melissa had a hidden battle raging in her mind and dream life that she was not able to overcome. She continually had dreams of one man she had previously been involved with. Thoughts of him unexpectedly flooded her mind throughout the day. She repented every time this occurred and even made renunciations out loud, but to no avail. The battle continued to rage.

Growing increasingly frustrated and concerned, Melissa set an appointment with her pastor and told him what was occurring. The pastor asked if she had broken all unholy soul ties with the man. Melissa had not heard this term before. The pastor explained that soul ties are emotional and spiritual connections that develop between those who jointly engage in sinful practices. These unholy alliances exert supernatural control over the individuals mentally, emotionally, and spiritually. The most common open door for allowing these ties to develop is sexual sin outside of marriage. They can also be established in an ungodly relationship in which emotional manipulation is used to control.

Melissa and her pastor spent time praying. He led her in a time of repentance concerning the unholy relationship she had engaged in. They broke and renounced all unholy soul ties in operation between her and this past boyfriend. The pastor then asked Melissa if she had kept old love letters or gifts from this person. Melissa thought for a few moments and remembered that she had a box of these items packed away in the attic. Per her pastor's instructions, when Melissa returned home, she climbed up in the attic and retrieved that box. She threw away the box of love letters and all the gifts she had received during that relationship. From that moment on, the dreams and thoughts about this man totally stopped!

A Lamp to the Soul

Jesus said in Matthew 6:22, "The eye is the lamp of the body. So if your eye is sound, your entire body will be full of light" (AMP). Let's look at the original meanings of several of the words in this verse. The Greek word for *lamp* is *luchnos*, which means "light or lamp showing the body which way to move or turn." *Sound* is translated from *haplous*, meaning "single-focused, simple, whole," and *light* comes from *photeinos*, which means "composed of light or of bright character." Understanding this, we see that our eyes show us the right way to go, enabling us to be singularly focused, simple, and whole. Then, as we move in a single, uncompromised, focused direction toward the things of God, we will walk in the light of our Father and show forth a bright, intelligent, cheerful character.

Jesus went on, "If your eye is unsound, your whole body will be full of darkness. If then the very light in you [your conscience] is darkened, how dense is that darkness!" (Matt. 6:23, AMP). Again, the original Greek words help us out here. The word for *unsound* here is *poneros*. It is defined as "evil, wicked, diseased, bringing a time full of peril to Christian faith" or "steadfastness." *Whole* comes from *holos*, meaning "throughout, all, and completely," and *darkened* is *skotos*, which means "darkened eyesight or blindness, ignorance with respect to divine things and human duties, and the accompanying ungodliness and immorality together with their consequent misery."

Basically, Jesus is saying this: If our eyes look upon that which is evil, then our entire being will be full of, or covered in, darkness. If the lamp in our conscience is darkened and diseased to things that will bring peril or trial to our Christian faith and steadfastness, we can then become ignorant of divine things, which will lead to ungodliness, immorality, and misery. Friends, our Lord is speaking a heavy word.

Before we continue, I want you to hear my heart. I realize that oftentimes teaching about what we are *not* to do can cause people to become overly suspicious, fearful, and legalistic. I am not promoting legalism. Nor do I want people to become suspicious or fearful in an unhealthy way. I am not telling everyone to get rid of their televisions or their computers. I do not believe this is what God is saying to us.

However, I do know that God wants us to be a reflection of His kingdom in this world. It is in my heart that each person reading this book will desire a close, pure, and holy relationship with our beautiful Savior. When we walk closely with Him, a passion for holiness will arise within us. There will be a deep, resounding cry that says we desire more of Him and no longer want the evil things of this world that cause us to be in mental and emotional bondage to strongholds of the enemy.

Could it be that the church and we as believers lack God's manifest presence, power, and love because of the things we allow into our beings through our choice of entertainment and the items we have in our homes? I will say this now: *we can have as much of God as we want.* To have more of Him, we must engage in an intentional pursuit of Him and make choices that will lead us into more of His glorious presence, anointing, and love.

Having said all this, what are the things we should avoid?

- TV shows, movies, and books steeped in perversion and sex

- Any and all pornographic material

- Perverse texting, better known as "sexting"

- Computer and online games steeped in violence, perversion, and witchcraft

- All things depicting and glorifying witchcraft, vampires, werewolves, séances, psychics, or demonic spirits

- Music and music videos that portray rebellion, evil, darkness, death, suicide, or perversion

- Horror movies

JOSHUA AND THE CHILDREN OF ISRAEL

After marching around Jericho again and again for a week and concluding with a final trumpet blast from the priests, Israel's army victoriously conquered the city. But before they even began their conquest, the Lord had given Israel very specific instructions about the taking of plunder: "Keep away from the devoted things, so that you will not bring about your own destruction by taking any of them. Otherwise you will make the camp of Israel liable to destruction and bring trouble on it" (Josh. 6:18).

After Israel's glorious victory, Joshua sent the troops out to fight the next town: Ai. Instead of having success this time, however, the Israelites suffered an embarrassing defeat that caused their hearts to melt like wax and robbed them of their faith. They were powerless and fearful.

As the leader of the people, Joshua wanted to know what had caused this drastic turn of events. He cried out to the Lord in prayer, and God promptly answered him:

> The Lord said to Joshua, Get up! Why do you lie thus upon your face?
>
> Israel has sinned; they have transgressed My covenant which I commanded them. They have taken some of the things devoted [for destruction]; they have stolen, and lied, and put them among their own baggage.
>
> That is why the Israelites could not stand before their enemies, but fled before them; they are accursed and have become devoted [for destruction]. I will cease to be with you unless you destroy the accursed [devoted] things among you.
>
> Up, sanctify (set apart for a holy purpose) the people, and say, Sanctify yourselves for tomorrow; for thus says the Lord, the God of Israel: There are accursed things in the midst of you, O Israel. You cannot stand before your enemies until you take away from among you the things devoted [to destruction].
> —JOSHUA 7:10–13, AMP

Those who are familiar with this story will remember that Achan had taken prohibited items from Jericho and hidden them among his own possessions (Josh. 6:19–21; 7:1). Achan's sin paralyzed the children of Israel and kept them from advancing. Imagine! One man's sinful choice affected the entire nation of Israel and prevented them from defeating their enemies and taking possession of their promised inheritance. We can learn a great lesson by this example: unacceptable and unpermitted possessions can leave us powerless to stand against our enemies.

TIME TO CLEAN HOUSE

Now that we understand that ungodly possessions can have a negative mental, emotional, spiritual, and physical impact on our lives, let's clean house! The following are steps in the purifying process.

Come before the Lord for a spiritual assessment.

Allow the Lord to lead this time as you come before Him. Let Him search you and speak to you just as David allowed Him to when he prayed: "Search me [thoroughly], O God, and know my heart! Try me and know my thoughts! And see if there is any wicked or hurtful way in me, and lead me in the way everlasting" (Ps. 139:23–24, AMP). Such an attitude is necessary because many times it is difficult for us to know our own hearts. When we truly listen to the Lord, we might learn that items we feel are permissible truly are not. If you are ready to be fully teachable in this process, it is also wise to ask the counsel of Christian family members, ministers, and trusted friends. They may have insight into things we should rid ourselves of.

Be sanctified.

Paul writes in 1 Thessalonians 5:23–24:

> May the God of peace Himself sanctify you through and through [separate you from profane things, make you pure and wholly consecrated to God]; and may your spirit and soul and body be preserved sound and

complete [and found] blameless at the coming of our Lord Jesus Christ (the Messiah).

Faithful is He Who is calling you [to Himself] and utterly trustworthy, and He will also do it [fulfill His call by hallowing and keeping you].

—AMP

The Greek word for *sanctify* in this passage is *hagiazo*. It means "to separate from profane things and dedicate to God, to cleanse externally and to purify internally by the renewing of the soul." Now is the time for us to be sanctified in the Lord—to take off the old and step into the new!

If the Lord reveals to you sinful thought patterns, behaviors, attitudes, and items you need to rid from your home, now is the time for you to repent. The Word of God tells us, "If we confess our sins, he is faithful and just and will forgive us our sins and purify us from all unrighteousness" (1 John 1:9).

Locate the defiled items and rid your home of them.

Now that you have invited the Lord into the spiritual assessment process, walk through your home and allow Him to show you the things that need to go. Once you have gathered the items, it is time to get rid of them. Many times you can simply throw them away. Sometimes, however, God may lead you to burn items such as pornographic material; satanic music; pagan objects; items associated with witchcraft, Freemasonry, or New Age meditation; and other dark things. Do not forget to include items from past sexual or ungodly relationships.

Commit to the process.

As we read above, the nation of Israel suffered a great setback because Achan took forbidden plunder for himself. Once Joshua discovered this, repented, and cleansed the people, he and the children of Israel were able to stand against their enemy, Ai, and obtain a complete victory (Josh. 8).

My husband and I so believe in this process that we do a spiritual housecleaning once a year and any other time the Lord leads us to do so. I am not talking about removing profane items, which I hope were all removed early on in our faith. I am speaking rather of those things that might present a hindrance in our time or relationship with the Lord. Allow me to explain.

As believers, we are always to be growing and maturing in our spiritual walk. What may have been acceptable a year ago may not be so now. The Lord may ask you to go a year without watching a certain television show and to read the Word of God at that time instead. Or maybe for a season the Lord will prompt you to lay down a hobby that requires a significant amount of your time. Sometimes He may ask you to abstain from certain foods or to go into a season of fasting from all media.

I travel and teach nationally and internationally. Plus, I am a wife and a mother of three beautiful daughters. I really do not have time for a lot of extracurricular activities or hobbies. But, like most women, I do enjoy a trip to the salon or spa. For years I enjoyed manicures and pedicures. In a prayer time a year ago, I felt the Lord asking me to lay this down for a season and to use that time for worship, prayer, and further study of the Bible. I gladly agreed, and I will not go back to regular appointments until I feel the Lord's release for me to do so. Now, God does want us to have fun and enjoyment, but there are seasons during which He asks us to give up possessions or lay down activities so that we can draw even closer to Him.

Renounce the enemy!

Break all sinful and unholy alliances made with the enemy, whether you made them willingly or unwillingly, knowingly or unknowingly. If you need to repent and break all unholy soul ties from past relationships, now is the time to do so. Use the prayer at the end of this chapter as a guide in doing this.

Set yourself and your property apart to the Lord.

Welcome the presence, love, and peace of the Lord to fill your home. I strongly suggest you walk the perimeter of your property and anoint its corners with anointing oil. As you welcome God's presence into your home and property, the Lord may highlight specific scriptures in your mind. When He does, write these verses on wooden stakes and drive them into the four corners of your property. Such actions are referred to as prophetic acts, which are deeds done to symbolize or respond to a prophetic word of the Lord. Driving stakes marked with Scripture into the four corners of your property is a way of consecrating your land, property, home, and family to the Lord.

SET FREE AND HEALED

Greg and I had been teaching an all-day seminar. As we made our way out of the meeting room, the pastor at whose church we were preaching asked if we would be willing to minister to Missy, a sweet nine-year-old girl. He explained that she had been greatly tormented in her mind, her dreams, and her physical body. We agreed to see the girl and were led back to the office, where Missy and her mother were waiting.

We were introduced to Missy and her mother, Lori, and began inquiring into the situation. Lori said that for six months Missy had been tormented by fear and plagued by terrifying nightmares, and she had chronic stomach pain that the doctors had not been able to diagnose. I asked Missy if something had occurred to cause this. She thought for a short time and replied, "Miss Becca, I had a really scary dream. In that dream a really big snake came up to me and bit me in my stomach. It keeps coming to me in my dreams to scare me. Even when I am awake I see that snake, and I am scared. My tummy has been hurting since that first dream. It is hurting really bad right now!"

"Missy," I told her, "we can pray and cause this pain to go away. Before we do, can Miss Becca ask you a question? Have you ever prayed and asked Jesus to come into your heart and be your Savior?"

Lori and Missy both contemplated that question and had the same response, "No, this has not happened."

Greg and I led Missy in receiving Jesus as her Savior. She quickly smiled, "Miss Becca, I feel so calm and happy!" But soon tears came to her eyes, and she grabbed her mother's hand and exclaimed, "My tummy is hurting really bad, Mama!" Greg and I knew at that point that there was still an open door for this child to be experiencing this type of mental torment and physical pain. We continued to pray.

Soon the Lord prophetically showed me a bookcase full of horror movies that were steeped in violence and witchcraft. I asked Lori if Missy was allowed to watch these types of movies. Lori quickly responded, "No, we do not allow her to watch things that will frighten her."

"Well, Lori, I feel that the Lord is showing me a bookcase full of horror movies. Why am I seeing this? Does someone in your home watch these movies?"

It was as if a light bulb came on in Lori's mind. "Why, yes! My husband loves horror movies, and he has a bookcase full of them. But we do not allow Missy to watch them."

Greg and I explained that even though Missy was not permitted to view these types of movies, having them in their home was still an open door for her mental torment, bad dreams, and physical attacks. We made it clear that we could pray for Missy and see her set free but that all those movies had to be taken out of the home and preferably destroyed. Lori agreed to speak with her husband about it as soon as they returned home.

Being led by the Lord, Greg and I prayed that all fear, mental torment, nightmares, and physical pain would be cancelled from Missy's life. Any witchcraft and death that were attached to those films tormenting Missy were renounced. We then welcomed God's healing power and love. Missy began to giggle, which soon led to laughter. "All the pain in my tummy is gone! I am not scared anymore, Mama! It feels so good!" We all rejoiced in her freedom.

That evening, when Lori and Missy returned home, Missy's father, Chris, was elated to see his little girl pain free. Lori explained to him all that had happened. Chris and Lori repented for allowing these types of movies in their home and for the resulting torment that their beautiful Missy had been subjected to. He quickly rid their home of all the horror movies. The movies were thrown into a dumpster. Chris and Lori renounced all witchcraft and death and welcomed the presence of the Lord into their home. From that night forward little Missy was no longer in mental torment. Her nightmares stopped, and her pain did not return.

Paul teaches us in Romans 12:2, "Don't become so well-adjusted to your culture that you fit into it without even thinking. Instead, fix your attention on God" (THE MESSAGE). Friends, I love Jesus. I love our heavenly Father. It is my heart to always be in hot pursuit of Him and to have a heart, life, and home that are consumed by Him. God wants our minds, our character, and our homes to be totally transfigured and completely changed for the better so that we are positioned and empowered to live a life pleasing and acceptable to Him. If we want this transformation, we must be ruthless in ensuring the enemy and any spiritually compromising beliefs and activities do not feel at home with us and in us. Take the time now to seek the Lord, repent, and rid your home of defiled things. Welcome in His awesome presence, and rejoice that your home is now set apart as a place of habitation for the presence of the Lord.

LET'S CLEAN HOUSE AND HEART

Lord, I confess that my possessions have at times shown that my priorities are not right before You. I have had _____ [list any items that you have or have had in your possession or in your home that you need to confess to the Lord] *in my life, and I know now that I must get rid of everything that hinders my relationship with You or creates a stronghold in my life.*

My eyes have looked at things that have created bondage in my life. I have kept devoted items for myself. Right now I commit to search for, give up, and destroy, if necessary, anything that hinders the free flow of Your Holy Spirit in my life.

I ask that You forgive me for the relationship I had with _____. *Thank You, Lord, for Your forgiveness. Right now in Jesus's name I renounce and break all unholy soul ties between myself and* _____.

Search me, Lord, and show me anything and everything in my life that needs to go. I want to be sanctified. I want to live a victorious life in Christ. I commit today to keep my house and my life clean of anything that dishonors You or opens a door to the enemy's working. My property belongs to You.

Thank You, Lord, for Your glorious freedom! In Jesus's name, amen.

Chapter 8

SPEAK WORDS OF
LIFE AND BLESSING

Words kill, words give life; they're either poison or fruit—you choose.

[PROVERBS 18:21, THE MESSAGE]

WORDS ARE OUR means of communication. They are everywhere, all the time! They are on television, in books, on the radio, in conversations, on billboards, on food products, in the media, in music. Recent studies reveal that on average both men and women speak around sixteen thousand words a day.[1] Personally, I love words, and I love to interact with others. I absolutely love people and enjoy having what my husband jokingly refers to as the gift of gab. In fact, I never lack a desire to engage in a great conversation.

My husband and my friends will attest to the fact that I can even carry on a conversation with myself. Many times I do exactly that. The funny thing is, I am usually unaware I am doing this until someone starts to laugh while watching me have a discussion all by myself. I have heard it said that this is a sign of genius. I don't know whether that is true, but if it is, I definitely choose to believe that report!

As we have discussed throughout this book, our brains are very active. Most research indicates that on average we think seventy thousand thoughts daily.[2] Numerous studies reveal that 80 percent of what we think about contains some sort of negative content.[3] For many, those negative thoughts create negative realities, because what we think on becomes a blueprint for our words and actions.

I was very intrigued by the idea that we have so many thoughts running through our heads each day, and I decided to try an experiment on myself. I sat in our comfy recliner all alone with my morning coffee in hand. The house was completely quiet. In that total silence I purposefully tried to sit quietly without engaging my mind. Soon I realized that even though my mouth was not opening, plenty of thoughts and words were forming in my mind. What was I going to do today? What awesome thing was God going to do that day for our ministry? How were our three daughters doing as they prepared that morning for their college classes? I needed to remember to call them and check on them. Oh, I had to do laundry, and I needed to pick up my dry cleaning before I flew out to my next speaking engagement the following day. Had Greg remembered to return those phone calls yesterday? I needed to write that article...I think by now you get the picture. Even though I was sitting completely silent, I can assure you that my mind was racing—and my thoughts were full of words.

TO INVOKE BLESSINGS

Our heavenly Father understands the significance of words. Actually, words are so important to our Lord that He speaks and releases blessings in each of our lives. These include the blessing of eternal salvation, the blessing of our kingdom inheritance as His sons and daughters, words of hope and life found in His Word, words of promise and affirmation as we seek His face in prayer, prophetic words of destiny and purpose, and so on. The first action our Lord engaged in after creating Adam and Eve was to release the Father's blessing through words. The Bible says, "God blessed them: 'Prosper! Reproduce! Fill Earth! Take charge!'" (Gen. 1:28, THE MESSAGE).

The Hebrew word for *bless* in this scripture is *barak*. It means "consecrated, set apart, sacred, holy, sanctified, and worthy of adoration, reverence or worship." It also means "to commend, to speak words invoking divine and supreme favor with the intent of favorable circumstances; to speak words of excellence or to greet one another with positive verbal exchanges." We see this pattern of blessing throughout Scripture. The Lord blessed Noah, Abraham, and Moses. Abraham's son, Isaac, blessed his sons, as did Jewish fathers throughout Scripture. Jesus blessed the disciples. Paul blessed Timothy. The same is true for each of us, God's children. Blessing is intertwined with our kingdom inheritance. God has blessed us."

To be blessed signifies that God is present and involved in our lives. It means His hand is directing our affairs for a divine purpose. He speaks words of divine favor and blessing over those who live a life dedicated to God. Another way to say this is that God provides this kind of blessing to those who "live before the face of God." Blessedness, then, describes the condition of one who reveres God, lives a life steeped in Him, and follows all His ways. This person does not just look to God in spiritual or religious matters but in every matter. God is not just the most important part of this person's life—to this individual, He is the very reason for his life and existence. He is this person's loving, truthful, and wise Father. Friends, this is how we should be. God should be everything to us.

As Christians, to practically apply the truth of these blessings, we must entrust ourselves to the Lord in such a way that He is our life. We must lay down everything He asks us to for the cause of Christ and His kingdom, and we must walk, live, and speak out our agreement with God and His Word. Our kingdom inheritance is as sons and daughters who believe the promise of divine favor He has bestowed on us. When we do this, we are partnering with the fullness of His Father's blessing. We will walk in blessedness and, in turn, speak and act in such a way that the promises of God are made real in our lives.

The Power of Negative Confession

While many of us know that God wants our lives to be blessed, that knowledge isn't always reflected in our words. The reality is that every one of us has spoken negatively about ourselves or others. And generally, before we even speak these negative words audibly, we have already rehearsed them repeatedly in our minds. This is significant, because what we believe to be true and what we think about consistently we eventually speak out—and ultimately, our words are then mirrored back to us in our experience.

This, of course, becomes a catch-22. Our negative thoughts become negative words, which become negative experiences—which results in our using more negative words. For instance, we say things such as: "I'm fat." "I'm not smart." "I'll never get out of this horrible situation." "We'll never be able to get financially ahead." "I'm poor." "No one likes me." "I'm tired." "I want to give up." "She's always mean." "He hates me." "It's everyone else's fault that my life is filled with pain." "God doesn't love me." "These negative things that are happening are just a part of life—nothing can change them, including God." We may think we're just stating the reality of the situation, but the more these kinds of words are repeated, the more we will find ourselves in the very situations bringing us so much frustration.

The Word of God is frank about our need to discipline our tongue and our speech:

> A bit in the mouth of a horse controls the whole horse.
> A small rudder on a huge ship in the hands of a skilled
> captain sets a course in the face of the strongest winds.
> A word out of your mouth may seem of no account,
> but it can accomplish nearly anything—or destroy it!

It only takes a spark, remember, to set off a forest
fire. A careless or wrongly placed word out of your
mouth can do that. By our speech we can ruin the
world, turn harmony to chaos, throw mud on a reputation, send the whole world up in smoke and go up in
smoke with it, smoke right from the pit of hell.

This is scary: You can tame a tiger, but you can't
tame a tongue—it's never been done. The tongue runs
wild, a wanton killer. With our tongues we bless God
our Father; with the same tongues we curse the very
men and women he made in his image. Curses and
blessings out of the same mouth!

My friends, this can't go on.

—James 3:5–10, The Message

My family lives in Colorado Springs near the Black Forest
area. You may have read or heard about the fire that sparked
and rapidly spread out of control in the summer of 2013. The
flames grew so intense that the headline of one local news-
paper read: "Unstoppable!"

Our home is located in the area that was put on manda-
tory evacuation. I can sincerely say that it was very intimidating when the fires reached a half mile from our home.
The image of flames leaping from treetop to treetop and the
looming black smoke making its way toward our neighborhood did not bring us a feeling of peace. Nor, as my husband,
Greg, says, did the many police officers who converged on
our neighborhood, telling us, "Get out now!"

From one spark that fire spread through thousands of
acres and was unstoppable for many days. But thanks to
the fearless firefighters and the power of prayer combined
with the belief that God would send rain, which He did,
those fires went from unstoppable to contained within two
days. Thankfully, our home and neighborhood were spared,

but tragically, roughly five hundred homes were destroyed before the fire was contained.

I realize that this is a graphic image, but this is the type of picture James is painting in the passage quoted previously. The truth is, our words carry great power. The Greek word for *curse* is *katara*. It means "the power to harm." To put it another way, *curse* is defined as "the heartfelt invoking or angry calling down of evil on oneself or another." If we repeatedly make negative confessions about ourselves or others, then whether we realize it or not, our words become flames that are difficult to extinguish, and these repeated spoken words are empowered to affect us in detrimental ways. Brenda's story clearly illustrates this point:

> For years I battled the accusation that I didn't care. I am a wife, mother, and grandmother as well as a leader in ministry. But over and over through the years, people told me, "You don't care." Every time I heard it, my heart broke. I sought the Lord, repented, and asked Him to give me His compassion for people and to help me to care more. Yet I continued to hear this comment.
>
> Each time someone told me I didn't care, I had to battle through another wave of deep discouragement. It didn't seem to matter what I did—I couldn't seem to get the victory over my inability to make people feel that I cared for them. I had been through many sessions of deliverance and inner healing, but at some point after each one, this issue always rose again, and I would go through another cycle of crying out to the Lord for breakthrough.
>
> Recently, I had to work with some young ladies on a ministry plan. I was in the unfortunate position of having to share some things with them that were really tough. Guess what? After the meeting the report came back, "It's like she doesn't care." They had no idea how much I had prayed about how I would present the

information to them. I had known that what I had to share would be disappointing to them and not the response they were expecting. I had known that if I didn't handle the situation right, my comments would be discouraging to them. So you can only imagine how devastated I was to hear that what they got out of our meeting was that I didn't care. One more time around the mountain.

Later that day I sat down with one of my pastors and asked her if I would ever be free from this. The pastor told me there had to be some root somewhere if this kept happening. She then asked me if I could remember when this had first started. All of a sudden a tsunami of emotions flooded me as the Lord took me back to my childhood. As if it was a movie, the memory played across my mind. I was thirteen years old and sitting on the steps of my school. My father had died just hours before. I had watched him battle brain cancer. I had more emotions than I knew what to do with, and I had no idea how to process everything. I had not been raised in anything remotely like a Christian environment to help support me throughout this process. I was hurting so badly, but instead of letting people bring me comfort, I built a wall of self-protection.

A friend and teacher of mine had come to me that morning and tried to comfort me. She told me how sorry she was and that she couldn't begin to understand my loss and pain. The Lord then reminded me of my response to this person. As a wounded young girl, the only thing I could think to say was that I didn't care and that I was glad my father was dead. Of course, I wasn't glad, and I did care. The truth was that I was glad I didn't have to watch my daddy suffer anymore. However, in this moment of traumatic loss and grief, my thoughts and words opened the door for a stronghold to ultimately attach itself to me. The Lord in His compassion had taken me to the exact moment that mind-set had entered in. Thirty-seven years later I was able to repent and pray through all the emotions and lies I had been bound by, and I finally received the victory!

FAITH COMES BY HEARING

The Word of God says, "The mouth speaks what the heart is full of" (Matt. 12:34). It is important that we review our thoughts and emotional attitudes each day. We must not let our thoughts or negative emotions take charge of us, because when we do, we sooner or later voice the ungodly beliefs that have influenced our hearts or the lies the enemy has placed in our minds. In doing this, we establish strongholds.

You might be asking, "Are you suggesting that because of my repeated negative confessions I have cursed myself or someone else? Could a stronghold now be rooted in me?" Maybe or maybe not. As Brenda shared in her testimony, the enemy took complete advantage of the trauma she experienced at the loss of her father, and one comment that she made in her pain eventually became a stronghold that lasted into her adult life. I cannot comment on each individual situation and whether a stronghold has taken root, but I will say this: many times we suffer great conflict and confusion in our lives because we have so critically judged others and spoken negatively concerning them.

Romans 10:17 tells us, "Faith comes by hearing, and hearing by the word of God" (MEV). Faith is a conviction that something is true and reliable. When something is audibly spoken numerous times, whether positive or negative, faith, or a belief, is built upon those words. And as we have said, our beliefs affect our actions. Let's look at some scriptures that show how our words influence our conduct:

Death and life are in the power of the tongue, and those who love it will eat its fruit.

—PROVERBS 18:21, MEV

There is one who speaks like the piercings of a sword, but the tongue of the wise brings health.

—PROVERBS 12:18, MEV

The truthful lip will be established forever, but a lying tongue is but for a moment.

—PROVERBS 12:19, MEV

Keep your tongue from evil, and your lips from speaking deceit. Turn away from evil, and do good; seek peace, and pursue it.

—PSALM 34:13–14, MEV

A man's stomach will be satisfied with the fruit of his mouth; and with the increase of his lips will he be filled.

—PROVERBS 18:20, MEV

The Lord GOD has given me the tongue of the learned, that I may know how to sustain him who is weary with a word.

—ISAIAH 50:4, MEV

Walk in wisdom toward those who are outside, wisely using the opportunity. Let your speech always be with grace, seasoned with salt, that you may know how you should answer everyone.

—COLOSSIANS 4:5–6, MEV

The mouth of the righteous is a fountain of life, but the mouth of the wicked conceals violence.

—PROVERBS 10:11, NAS

A wholesome tongue is a tree of life, but perverseness in it crushes the spirit.

—PROVERBS 15:4, MEV

Pleasant words are as a honeycomb, sweet to the soul and health to the bones.

—PROVERBS 16:24, MEV

Heaviness in the heart of man makes it droop, but a good word makes it glad.

—Proverbs 12:25, mev

A soft answer turns away wrath, but grievous words stir up anger.

—Proverbs 15:1, mev

He who guards his mouth preserves his life, but he who opens wide his lips will have destruction.

—Proverbs 13:3, mev

Whoever guards his mouth and his tongue keeps his soul from troubles.

—Proverbs 21:23, mev

The heart of the righteous studies to answer, but the mouth of the wicked pours out evil things.

—Proverbs 15:28, mev

Set a guard, O Lord, over my mouth; keep watch over the door of my lips.

—Psalm 141:3, mev

In reading these verses, it is clear that our words have consequences that can be either good or bad. On the one hand, we see that when we do not properly express ourselves either in the words we speak or in the manner in which we speak those words, great harm can result. Here are some of the negative consequences of not disciplining our words revealed in the previous verses:

- Words can bring death.

- Rash words can cut like a sword.

- Lying words will not last but are short-lived.

- Wicked words bring violence.

- Perverse words crush the spirit.

- Anxiety and words of anxiousness bring depression.

- Harsh words stir up anger.

- Speaking unwise words can bring ruin.

- When we do not guard our speech with wisdom, our souls come into great unrest and turmoil.

- The wicked mouth pours out evil.

On the positive side, however, we see that if we choose to speak words of kingdom life and blessing, we can start a kingdom fire, igniting a passion for God's glory that will not be extinguished. Following are some of the benefits and blessings that can result when we speak scripturally about ourselves and others:

- Life and good fruit come from our words.

- Wise words bring healing.

- Truthful words live forever.

- Keeping our tongues from evil brings goodness and peace.

- Words produce life and satisfaction.

- The words of a disciple bring life to the weary.

- Wisdom and gracious speech will bless those we relate to.

- Righteous words bring a fountain of life.

- Soothing words bring life.

- Pleasant words bring healing to our souls and bones.

- Good words bring healing to anxious emotions.

- Gentle words turn away anger and wrath.

- Guarding our words preserves life.

- Guarding our words keeps our soul (mind, will, and emotions) from trouble.

- When we are walking in righteousness, we think on how to answer in wisdom and love.

- When we pray and ask the Lord to help us guard our words, He is faithful to teach us and to show us how to do it.

Friends, there is great power in our words. The words we speak and the way in which we communicate them have the ability to manipulate and control our own well-being and that of others. They have the capacity to hold a person in bondage or set them free. Words can bring death, or they can bring life, hope, purpose, and emotional well-being. We have the choice.

CHOOSING THE POWER OF BLESSING

If we want to have victory over our thoughts and our tongues, we must practice self-control. Refusing to confess negative words that kill and choosing to speak out the blessings in the Word of God produce a drastically transformed life.

Greg and I have been blessed with three beautiful daughters: Kendall, Rebecca, and Katie. Of course, as parents we are proud of all three of our girls. We believe for the Lord's best in their lives, and we have taught them since they were young the power of prayer and of speaking blessings (declaring the promises God made to us in His Word and the truth of our identity as His beloved children) out loud.

Throughout her junior and senior years in high school,

Katie (from whom I have full permission to share this story) struggled with thoughts of rejection and depression. Several boys in her school had chosen to treat Katie in a demeaning manner and to spread false rumors about her. Greg made sure to contact the parents of the boys to see this stopped, and we also informed the school counselor of what was occurring. Despite our stepping in as parents to protect our daughter, the negative words had already begun to adversely affect our precious Katie.

She soon began to make confessions such as, "I am not as pretty as the other girls. No one likes me. I am not as talented as my sisters." Knowing the power of forgiveness, we led her in a time of forgiving the boys and blessing them, although we certainly guided her not to hang out with this crowd of friends. We prayed for her, spoke blessings over her, and had her speak out words of affirmation and blessing. But to no avail. The enemy kept attempting to take advantage of this situation and to plant thoughts of rejection in her mind and heart.

One weekend Katie's older sister, Kendall, was home visiting from college. She could tell that Katie was once again in a battle. She and our other daughter, Rebecca, loved on Katie, spoke words of affirmation to her, and proceeded to write on her dresser mirror with yellow nail polish the truth about Katie:

> You are beautiful
> You are smart
> You are funny
> You are special
> Jesus loves you!

Kendall issued strict instructions to Katie to speak these words out loud every time her thoughts were flooded with the memory of the lies those boys had spoken against her. Suddenly, Katie was able to receive the truth, and she did exactly as Kendall had instructed her. For many days we could hear Katie from her bedroom speaking out the words of blessing and affirmation. Soon we witnessed Katie once again becoming the confident girl we knew her to be. Things began to change for the better in her life. She is now happy and excelling in college. To this day those words remain on her mirror as a reminder of the power of speaking out words of blessing and of her true kingdom identity.

What occurs when we choose to walk in the way of blessedness? What transpires when we speak out words that are in line with our kingdom inheritance of blessing? Demonic strongholds are cancelled, and strongholds of the mind and emotions are defeated. Negative thought patterns and harmful emotional cycles cease. Praise and celebration come forth in our hearts and minds.

Negative words release negative experiences. But speaking the truth of God's Word releases His blessings: It brings forth prosperity, happiness, and great joy. It invokes the divine favor of God. It releases great faith. It positions us for success. It causes gratefulness, thanksgiving, and praise to flow in us, through us, and out of us. It empowers us to function in loving kingdom relationships.

When we speak truth, we set an example that draws the lost world. People can see victory over strongholds in our lives, and they become hungry for the same blessed reality.

Let's Pray for Words That Bring Life

Lord, I confess that I have spoken negative words and curses about myself and others. I ask that You forgive me for believing and verbalizing the lies of the enemy. I know, Lord, that You make no mistakes and that I and those I have spoken against are fearfully and wonderfully made. Lord, forgive me for saying _____. [Allow the Lord to bring to mind those words that need to be washed under the cleansing and healing power of the blood of Jesus. Insert here the specific word curses that you have spoken. These might be personal in nature, or you may have spoken them toward another.] *I thank You, Lord, for Your forgiveness.*

In Jesus's name, I cancel the power of every destructive word that I have spoken, and I pray that You bless those of whom I have spoken negatively and critically. Lord, keep me from the temptation of speaking word curses. I welcome patience, love, joy, peace, self-control, wisdom, and gentleness into my thoughts, emotions, and speech. Let my words be a blessing to You, to me, and to those I encounter.

I declare that I choose Your report for my life. I am the head and not the tail. I am victorious. I am more than a conqueror. My words will bring life. I choose to walk in a blessed life with a renewed mind and healed emotions. Where the Spirit of the Lord is, there is freedom, and from this time forward I choose freedom and victory in my words! In Jesus's name, amen.

Chapter 9

RESOLVE TO WALK
IN FREEDOM

*Here's what I want you to do, God helping you: Take your everyday,
ordinary life—your sleeping, eating, going-to-work, and walking-
around life—and place it before God as an offering. Embracing
what God does for you is the best thing you can do for him. Don't
become so well-adjusted to your culture that you fit into it without
even thinking. Instead, fix your attention on God. You'll be
changed from the inside out. Readily recognize what he wants
from you, and quickly respond to it. Unlike the culture around
you, always dragging you down to its level of immaturity, God
brings the best out of you, develops well-formed maturity in you.*

[ROMANS 12:1–2, THE MESSAGE]

ONCE YOU HAVE realized freedom, you need to maintain it. The problem is, Satan is a sore loser, and he will attempt to bring temptation and to speak lies into your thought patterns to reopen a door of bondage in your life. Not only will this door be opened, but the wrong choices and bad habits from your past will also rise up to pull you back. It is important, however, that we *continue* to desire freedom and not give in to temptation or discouragement and end up quitting!

I shared in chapter 6 that my father passed into heaven in 2008. He was a great husband and father, and he always made sure that my mother, my sister, and I were taken care of. He had prepared a will many years before he passed away. Due to the closeness of my family, we were fully aware of my father's wishes and how his belongings were to be distributed. But what would have happened, hypothetically speaking, if during the reading of my father's will, a stranger had walked into the room and attempted to take the financial blessing left to my mom and the inheritance my father earmarked for my sister and me? Would I have allowed this to happen? Absolutely not!

I am known, as I mentioned previously, for having a bit of a feisty side. I can say without any doubt that the aggressive side of my personality would have definitely manifested in such a moment. I would not have been polite or courteous. That stranger would have been abruptly escorted out of the room, and the authorities would have been called. It is completely safe to say we would not have allowed a stranger, who had no right to our inheritance, to obtain it.

I shared this hypothetical scenario while I was teaching once in Arizona. I asked the group, "What do you think I would have done? What would each of you do in such a situation?" One lady unapologetically shouted from the audience, "I would punch that man in the nose!" Of course, everyone in the roomed laughed at her unexpected exclamation. Amused, I shouted in agreement, "Amen, sister! Punch him in the nose!"

Why am I sharing this? Because this is the same purposeful, energetic response we should have when the enemy, our flesh, and the world around us plot to steal the kingdom inheritance that God has designed for each of us! We need to be intentional and determined in our resolve not to allow what is rightfully ours as children of the King to be stolen.

DRAW NEAR TO GOD AND HE WILL DRAW NEAR TO YOU

I asked this question previously, but I am going to present it again: Do you believe the Lord loves you enough to set you free from trauma, hurt, and demonic strongholds? I want to

encourage you to believe that He most assuredly does. Paul
instructs us on this point in 2 Corinthians 3:18:

> Whenever, though, they turn to face God as Moses
> did, God removes the veil and there they are—face-
> to-face! They suddenly recognize that God is a living,
> personal presence, not a piece of chiseled stone. And
> when God is personally present, a living Spirit, that
> old, constricting legislation is recognized as obsolete.
> We're free of it! All of us! Nothing between us and
> God, our faces shining with the brightness of his face.
> And so we are transfigured much like the Messiah,
> our lives gradually becoming brighter and more beau-
> tiful as God enters our lives and we become like him.
> —THE MESSAGE

God not only wants us set free, He wants us to find that
freedom by encountering Jesus in His perfect, glorious,
kingly majesty so that we will become the reflection of His
resplendent, divine brightness. Friends, I can attest to the
truth that when we draw near to Jesus and encounter Him
personally in all His majestic holiness, He draws near to us,
and His light and love transform us. When that takes place,
nothing and no one can ever steal from us that supernatural
transformational moment. It becomes a defining moment in
our lives, one that affirms who we are and what we have
become: people captivated by the Father, spiritually on fire
for Him, and, from a place of deep sincere thankfulness,
totally committed to Him.

I shared a portion of my testimony in chapter 2. Because of
the choices I made when living in rebellion, when I returned
to the Lord, the enemy was able to torment me mentally
with guilt, shame, and condemnation. Even though I had
repented, turned from the sins that had consumed me, and
had totally committed myself to the Lord, I experienced an
intense battle in my mind. I could go to church, put on a

happy face, appear as if everything was good, and say all the accepted religious things: "I am well. I am blessed!" But behind closed doors, I experienced intense mental warfare. How could I be set free from the shameful thought patterns that I battled as a result of my past?

Constant accusations from the enemy raged in my thoughts: "You think you have been forgiven, but God will never forgive you for what you did. Your salvation can never be secure. Your Christian witness has been ruined!" The closer I drew to the Lord, the louder the enemy's tormenting voice grew. Greg prayed for and encouraged me, but I did not gain freedom. I suffered from a destructive stronghold of the mind, which caused my emotions and thoughts to become gripped by depression.

During this season, our oldest daughter was two and a half years old. From the time she was a baby, she had exhibited a strong sensitivity to the Lord. She saw visions and had dreams of angels. She had, and still has, a strong prophetic gift.

One afternoon, I laid her down for a nap and decided to do my Bible study while she slept. I vividly remember the battle in my mind being extremely intense that day. While reading the Bible, I cried out to God, "Lord, please help me!" I felt Him directing me to read about the woman with the issue of blood, so I turned to Mark 5:25-34.

The Lord prompted me to study what this woman had truly endured for twelve years. I learned that she had spent all her money seeking doctors for her cure. Nothing had worked. I discovered that Jewish law dictated that anyone who came in physical contact with her while she was bleeding would, like her, be labeled impure. Therefore, every time this woman went out in public, she had to announce out loud, "Unclean, unclean, unclean!"

This woman had not experienced any human physical

contact for the twelve-year period she had bled internally. Not only did she need a physical healing, but she needed the supernatural healing power of the Lord to break the years of word curses she had spoken out over herself. Many of us are familiar with the story. The woman pressed through the crowd, touched the hem of our Lord's garment, and was immediately healed.

When I realized the magnitude of what this woman had endured and the incredible healing she had received, I was emotionally overcome. I fell to my living room floor and began to cry out determinedly, "Lord, if You healed this woman with the issue of blood, You can heal me from this mental torment and depression. I am setting my face like flint, grabbing hold of the hem of Your garment, and not letting go until I am healed!"

As I drew near to the Lord, I felt His presence drawing near to me, but my shouting woke my daughter from her nap. In her two-year-old voice, she called to me, "Mommy, I wake up now. Mommy, I hungry!" After several minutes I succumbed to her calls, getting up from the floor and retrieving her from her bed.

I made her afternoon snack, a peanut-butter-and-jelly sandwich, and sat with her at the table while she enjoyed her treat. Soon I was aware that I had not yet received complete freedom. In my spirit I cried out, "Lord, I am not free yet." The voice of the enemy was screaming in my mind, "I told you that you will never be free. You cried out to God, and He did not answer you or heal you!" My depression, hopelessness, and despair were almost unbearable.

Suddenly Kendall began to laugh and joyfully exclaim, "Mommy, it so funny, it so funny!"

Not understanding, I replied, "Baby, what is so funny?"

"Mommy, don't you see, don't you see?"

"No, baby, I don't understand. What is it I am supposed to see?"

My two-year-old daughter climbed out of her booster seat and walked back and forth in front of me like a warrior. She was giggling and laughing in great joy. "Mommy, don't you see? It is Jesus and an angel, and they are here doing this for you!" As she continued her warrior march back and forth in front of me, I began to weep and said, "Lord, if You are here fighting for me, then I am going to enter the fight with You!"

That evening at church I rushed to the altar to speak with my home-group pastor. "Tonight is my night of freedom. Please pray for me." She undoubtedly saw that God was at work. She laid hands on my eyes and began to pray, "Lord, show her what You want her to see." As she prayed, the Lord imparted a vision to me. I saw two hands holding an ancient book. I knew the book was eternal and that the hands holding it were the Lord's. The book was opened to a page, and a bright light highlighted a small portion of the text. At first I could not read the writing, but the Lord brought the book closer, and the writing came clearly into focus. To my pleasure and astonishment, I realized the Lord was holding the Lamb's Book of Life and I saw written plainly in gold: "Rebecca Long Greenwood." I began to sob uncontrollably.

Another pastor, having made his way to the altar, laid hands on my eyes. He repeated the same prayer, "Lord, show her what You want her to see." Again, the Lord allowed me to see a vision. This time I saw Jesus. He was coming toward me with a smile on His face and the awesome, supernatural power of the wind of the Spirit enveloping Him. He looked at me and exclaimed in great love, holiness, and authority: "Becca, take up your cross and follow Me. It is over—it is finished!" Friends, at the moment those words were declared from my Jesus's mouth, that stronghold of mental torment and depression left. It was instantly gone. With great rejoicing, tears of thankfulness, and joy I rose victoriously free from the floor of the church altar, and I have not been depressed since that day. That was twenty-one years ago!

I know without any shadow of doubt that Jesus wants us free. He wants you free. If He can heal the woman with the issue of blood and can radically deliver me, He can set you free too! If you invite Him into your situation, He will show up, and He will deliver you! There is such incredible beauty and truth when God is personally present in our situation. In that divine moment when there is nothing between us and Him, He radically frees and transforms us.

If we want to maintain the victory we have found in our thoughts and emotions, now is the time for us to set our face like flint and to resolve to walk out the freedom we have obtained through Christ. Hebrews 12:1–3 exhorts us not to grow weary but to finish the race set before us:

> Do you see what this means—all these pioneers who blazed the way, all these veterans cheering us on? It means we'd better get on with it. Strip down, start running—and never quit! No extra spiritual fat, no parasitic sins. Keep your eyes on *Jesus*, who both began and finished this race we're in. Study how he did it. Because he never lost sight of where he was headed—that exhilarating finish in and with God— he could put up with anything along the way: Cross, shame, whatever. And now he's *there*, in the place of honor, right alongside God. When you find your- selves flagging in your faith, go over that story again, item by item, that long litany of hostility he plowed through. *That* will shoot adrenaline into your souls!
>
> —THE MESSAGE

No matter what we are facing, we can resolve to take personal responsibility for our spiritual life and to learn intentional steps we can take that will starve out strongholds and prevent them from gaining authority in our lives.

TAKING OUR THOUGHTS CAPTIVE

What are the steps we need to take to hold on to our freedom and walk daily in the victory God has promised us? Second Corinthians 10:5 says, "[We] refute arguments and theories and reasonings and every proud and lofty thing that sets itself up against the [true] knowledge of God; and we lead every thought and purpose away captive into the obedience of Christ (the Messiah, the Anointed One)" (AMP). Wrong thinking leads to wrong feeling, and when we indulge in wrong feeling, before long our heart and mind are pulled apart, and we are strangled by worry. In order for us to maintain freedom and victory in our ongoing faith walk, we need to gain control over our thought life so that negative thoughts do not control us or pull us down.

As we have learned, however, thoughts are real and powerful, even though they cannot be seen, weighed, or measured. How are we to handle the unwelcome thoughts that come to us?

Most people are bothered by marketers who call us at home in an attempt to sell us products over the phone. If we wanted or needed to purchase the item, we would do so, right? Why do these companies think they can call us at odd times in order to convince us to make a purchase? The phone call was not requested and is not welcomed. In order to stop the nuisance of these unsolicited callers, many of us check the caller ID before picking up the phone or we block unwanted or unknown numbers.

This is what we must do to stop thoughts placed in our minds by defeated strongholds. We do not want the thought, we did not ask for it, and we did not invite it in. Therefore, we do not need to pick up the receiver and entertain the sales pitch. When you receive these unwelcome thoughts, allow a righteous anger to arise in your spirit toward the lies of the enemy. Block the message from getting through, and command it to stop in Jesus's name.

My friend Lisa learned to do just that. I asked her to share her powerful testimony of how the Lord set her free and taught her to take her thoughts captive:

> For years I struggled with fear. It wasn't a fear of leaving the house or of speaking in public—the typical fears a person thinks of when he or she hears the word *fear*.
>
> This was a fear of my husband cheating on me. I struggled with this fear for most of my marriage, even though my husband had never cheated on me or done anything to betray me in any way. I would entertain a thought such as, "What if my husband *has* cheated on me?" Then that thought would turn into another thought, and before I knew it, I really believed that he was being unfaithful. I was gripped with fear about this, and it caused me a lot of anxiety and depression. It took a toll on my marriage as well, because my husband had this wife who didn't trust him.
>
> I was in bondage to this fear, and no matter how much I read Scripture and prayed, I couldn't get the deliverance that I needed to be set free. I needed guidance on how to fight this, but since I was embarrassed to talk to anybody about it and ask for prayer, I suffered for years. But I knew that I couldn't go on living this way, so at last I went to Becca and her team. I finally received the deliverance and healing from God that I had prayed for. One key spiritual practice I learned in the process is that I had to take those thoughts captive as the Word of God says to do.
>
> After my deliverance the thoughts of fear tried to enter from time to time, but I immediately took those thoughts captive and said out loud, "My husband loves

me. He is faithful to me. I refuse to listen to the lies of the enemy." I also had to be conscious of what I watched on television and read. I couldn't allow television shows, radio programs, or articles that dealt with infidelity as entertainment to put ideas in my mind.

Like Lisa, we need to refuse thoughts that would return us to bondage and determine to align our thinking with the Word of God. For the remainder of this chapter, we are going to examine a number of ways we can deliberately reject negative thought patterns and walk in freedom from strongholds.

Be patient with yourself

Do not become harsh with and critical of yourself as you learn to change your thought patterns. If you begin to think on the lies of a broken stronghold, repent as soon as you become aware. Let repentance become a lifestyle so nothing has a chance to take root. Keep moving forward in your freedom. Do not grow impatient as you are learning new ways to think.

Remain steadfast in faith

Upon resolving to walk out this new freedom, we must remain steadfast in faith and press toward the call God has for us. Victory does not mean everything in our lives will be perfect. We will still have times of adversity and trial. In these times do not become complacent. Don't fall into the trap of rehearsing the past or thinking about your current situation. Doing this will cause your faith to become inactive, which will open the door to fear, anxiety, doubt, and confusion. Believe the Lord and His promises. Trust His faithfulness and goodness. Allow your faith to be stirred and strengthened by speaking and doing the Father's will.

Guard against spiritual laziness

Hebrews 6:12 tells us that we should "not grow disinterested and become [spiritual] sluggards, but imitators, behaving as do those who through faith (by their leaning of the entire personality on God in Christ in absolute trust and confidence in His power, wisdom, and goodness) and by practice of patient endurance and waiting are [now] inheriting the promises" (AMP). The word for *sluggard* here implies laziness and slowness to learn. We are to shrug off the immaturity of past seasons, focus on our promised kingdom inheritance, and embrace it for our future.

Do not grow careless

Do not grow careless in your choices of entertainment. Be faithful to the new season you are walking in by choosing healthy forms of entertainment. Consistently practice the spiritual housecleaning action steps discussed in chapter 7.

Build healthy relationships

As you enter into this new season of victory, it would be wise for you to assess your friendships. Do not be surprised if the Lord leads you to establish new relationships. Oftentimes in order for us to go into a new season, we have to let go of the past one. It might be time for you to distance yourself from unhealthy and ungodly relationships. Ask the Lord to give you new relationships that are pure, uplifting, and encouraging.

Stay in the Word of God

What a joy it is to sit before the pages of the Bible, the Spirit-inspired Word of God, and let the Holy Spirit reveal God's truth. It has the power to revolutionize our thinking and transform our lives. We read in the Book of Hebrews:

> The Word that God speaks is alive and full of power
> [making it active, operative, energizing, and effective];

> it is sharper than any two-edged sword, penetrating
> to the dividing line of the breath of life (soul) and the
> [the immortal] spirit, and of joints and marrow [of
> the deepest parts of our nature], exposing and sifting
> and analyzing and judging the very thoughts and
> purposes of the heart.
> —HEBREWS 4:12, AMP

The Word of God is quick, alive, powerful, and active. It is like a double-edged sword that is far-reaching in its effects. It reaches down into all of our parts and functions and issues verdicts on what is uncovered within us. It penetrates even to the innermost secrets and motives of our hearts, which are hidden from our consciousness and from the eyes and ears of other people. Simply put, God's Word brings to light issues that we are unaware of.

I suggest that you make time every day to read and meditate on the Word. Follow a regular schedule in your reading, and give yourself time to pray, think, and meditate. Let the Spirit of God help you search the Word and teach you. Allow a hunger for the Bible to come alive in you. Spending time in the Word of God should be a priority for you. It can transform your life.

Worship God

Spending time worshipping the Lord causes us to rise above the circumstances we face and enter into God's glorious light and presence. Enjoying the presence of God and honoring Him in worship is paramount. Rushing into His presence and begging for peace of mind will never produce results. We must bow before Him in worship and let Him search our hearts and minds. It is in the intimate place of worship that we are able to quiet our souls, get our emotions and thoughts under the authority of our spirits, and hear the voice of the Lord. This gives us the strength to press forward and move ahead in the peace of the Lord with the assurance of freedom and victory.

As you worship the Lord, I suggest that you speak the names of God out loud. This will remind you of who He is and of His power, which will further strengthen your faith. The following is a brief list of some of His names to help you start this process:

- Yahweh
- The Alpha and the Omega (the Beginning and the End)
- The Cornerstone
- The Redeemer of the world
- The lover of my soul
- The risen Lamb
- Most holy One
- Faithful Father
- Master
- Teacher
- Jehovah
- The Rose of Sharon
- Merciful Lord
- Elohim
- The great Shepherd
- The God of covenant
- Heavenly Father
- Messiah

- The light of the world
- Breath of heaven
- Son of Man
- Son of God
- The Comforter
- The One full of majesty
- Glorious One
- Emmanuel

Raise your voice in adoration, and sing to the Lord. Sing new songs of His beauty and faithfulness. Allow yourself to express your love and gratitude to Him in new ways that remind you of a new facet of our God. Worship is one of the most powerful weapons of warfare that we have!

Give praise and thanks to the Lord

Praise is an outward expression of an inward attitude. As you seek to turn from wrong thought patterns and embrace right thinking, having a heart and an attitude of praise, gratitude, and thanksgiving will help you immeasurably. We are going to discuss in depth in chapter 10 how to think on things that are good and to speak the truth of God's goodness. But I do want to state here the importance of declaring the positive things God is doing for you and thanking Him for His faithfulness. When we taste and see that the Lord is good, praise, thanksgiving, and rejoicing should be a natural response.

Spend time in prayer

As we spend time before the Lord developing a prayer life, we draw closer to Him and to His desires and plans for our lives. As we do this, our thoughts come more and more into line with God's thoughts, and we are strengthened to refuse old patterns of thinking. Are there times in which our flesh will not want to come before the Lord and pray? Yes. But I want to exhort you to make time for prayer, even when you do not feel like praying. Be faithful to your prayer life.

There are times when circumstances have sapped my desire to worship or pray. But when I choose even in those times to pull away from the busyness and distractions to worship and pray, God's presence begins to flood over me, and I feel His peace. It is in this place of praying and seeking Him that we are spiritually transformed and we become an expression of who God is. The Lord makes us secure in our identity as His children and in His awesome protection, and this gives us the confidence to stand in the midst of trial, temptation, and attack from the enemy.

Engage in seasons of fasting

Often in God's Word we see that when a person needed a supernatural breakthrough or cried out to the merciful, sovereign God, he or she was not just praying but also fasting. We too can benefit from this practice as we learn to walk steadfastly in our newfound freedom in Christ. I appreciate what Cindy Jacobs wrote in *Possessing the Gates of the Enemy*: "Fasting multiplies the effect of prayer at least several times.... Fasting will touch things that prayer alone will not affect."[1]

Fasting is not a Christian diet. Nor is it a means of changing *God*; it is about changing *us* so we can come into agreement with the Lord and His plans—and stay aligned with Him. When we hunger for more, we will receive more. When we hunger for God, He will fill us.

Fasting brings many spiritual benefits. It is an act of setting ourselves aside solely for the Lord, and it teaches us to deny our flesh so that we can receive more of Him. It empowers our praying and increases our spiritual discernment. It positions us to hear and recognize God's heart, voice, and timing more clearly. In the process of denying our flesh, fasting brings us into a greater level of humility. Our faith is increased as we discover that we do not live by bread alone. Fasting positions us to see victory in battles and in what seem to us impossible situations. When we fast, we experience breakthrough against darkness.

In Matthew chapter 6 Jesus names three things that believers should do: "When you pray...when you give...when you fast" (Matt. 6:2, 5, 16). He doesn't say "if" but "when." If we can find the time to pray and give, we as believers can also find the time to fast.

Make things right

We have discussed repentance and forgiveness extensively in this book, but sometimes, in order for us to gain complete freedom, repentance is not enough. Sometimes restitution also needs to be made. Did the sin you committed and/ or the resulting stronghold violate or harm another individual? If so, then you need to make things right. Refusing to do so will most certainly hinder your ability to walk in the fullness of freedom.

The principle of restitution is one that we rarely discuss in today's culture. It is an important but simple principle that safeguards our relationships with one another and with the Lord. Even when something is done by mistake, we should make restitution for the loss we have caused.

The Lord spoke to Moses in Numbers 5:5–7: "Tell the People of Israel, When a man or woman commits any sin, the person has broken trust with GOD, is guilty, and must confess the sin. Full compensation plus twenty percent must be made to whoever was wronged" (THE MESSAGE). Do you have outstanding financial obligations that you have not met, forgotten about, or even blatantly ignored? These need to be paid. Not all things can be corrected, but if the Lord is consistently reminding you of something that needs to be rectified, it is important for you to obey Him.

Not only are we to make restitution, but maybe it is time for us to *receive* restitution from all the places the enemy has stolen or robbed from us—places where we have planted financial or spiritual seed but have seen no harvest. What do I mean? Sometimes our hope is deferred and we become discouraged and confused because we have prayed and believed so long for a breakthrough—but we haven't seen one. We need to pray in faith, press in to the promises God has given us, and break the assignment of the enemy that is designed to withhold divine promises so that we can receive restitution.

Our oldest daughter, Kendall, learned this in a personal way in her first semester of her junior year in college. For the previous two years she had received grants, work study, and other financial assistance that proved to be a great blessing. She loved her college, her classes, and her job working for the dean of journalism. She was thriving.

Suddenly, Kendall received a letter in the mail from the financial aid department. It stated that a mistake had been made in granting her the awards she had received during her first two years in college and that she would no longer be awarded grants, work study, or assistance for the remainder of her college years.

She was devastated. Her father and I were not pleased. We called and spoke with the head of the financial aid department several times, each phone call lasting a minimum of two hours. The woman explained that the department had in error granted Kendall awards for which she was not eligible. She went on to say, "You and your husband should be grateful for the help Kendall received during her first two years on campus. And you should be very thankful we are not requiring you to pay back to the university what we previously allotted to her."

As a result of this decision, Kendall withdrew from her classes that semester and began online courses to complete her degree in journalism. She was greatly discouraged. We explained to her, "Kendall, we do not know how, but God is going to work a miracle on your behalf. We have to pray in faith."

Greg and I were not happy and felt that we needed the prayers of many intercessors. We asked our prayer partners to pray in agreement with us. We as a family also prayed. We believed for God's promises on Kendall's life, broke all warfare assignments of the enemy against her future calling and career in writing, and believed that in every way she had been robbed financially, restitution would be made. Within two months Kendall received another "suddenly." It was a second letter from the financial aid department granting her the same awards she had received during her previous two years. There were no apologies to her or to us, nor any explanation of why things had totally changed. To our delight Kendall finished her remaining one and a half years of college without any further denials.

If you want to reject the lies of the enemy and the strongholds of your past, you must be ready to make restitution in any area in which you owe something, and you must be ready to receive restitution in those areas where the enemy has stolen something from you.

Remain teachable

One key ingredient to maintaining victory is to remain teachable in your heart, mind, and soul. Listen to anointed and gifted Bible teachers; their messages can help keep you on focus. Surround yourself with others who are walking out a life of humility and freedom, and glean from them. Attend church and Bible studies on a regular basis.

Live a life of integrity

As believers, we are called to lead lives of integrity. We should walk in an upright manner. Our yes should be yes, and our no should be no. When we give our word, we should keep it. Our personal lives should exemplify sound and biblical handling of finances and strong family relationships.

The apostle Paul wrote: "Show your own self in all respects to be a pattern and a model of good deeds and works, teaching what is unadulterated, showing gravity [having the strictest regard for truth and purity of motive], with dignity and seriousness" (Titus 2:7, AMP). Those who live lives of integrity are honest and sincere, with pure motives. They are not self-seeking, and they are characterized by the love and good deeds of the Father.

As you determine to walk out your faith and to maintain freedom and victory in your life, the Lord will help you to grow in each of these areas and to continually change you from glory to glory.

LET'S PRAY FOR THE POWER TO WALK IN FREEDOM

Lord, I rejoice in this new beginning of freedom in my life. Thank You for the awesome gift of being liberated by You. I embrace the work You are doing in me, and I accept all that You have for my life.

I choose to keep my eyes, vision, and focus on You, Jesus. Help me to set my face like flint and to run the race You have set before me. I speak to my mind and my thoughts, and I tell them to stay focused on and captivated with the Lord. God, protect me, my mind, and my emotions from vain imaginations, lies of the enemy, and demonic strongholds. I choose to live a life founded on prayer, based on the Word of God, and saturated in worshipping, praising, and exalting You.

I love You, Lord. You are an awesome, magnificent, faithful, all-powerful, loving God. Fill me, Holy Spirit, with Your presence, and guide and direct me to lead a humble, teachable life of kingdom integrity. And God, I ask for personal encounters with You. Jesus, I want to know You more. I ask that You show Yourself to me in ways that I have not known. I welcome You to speak to me and to show Yourself to me. I want to know You more. Transform me. I love You, Lord. Amen.

Chapter 10

THINK ON WHAT IS GOOD

If there be any virtue, and if there be any praise, think on these things.

[PHILIPPIANS 4:8, ASV]

I F WE WANT to experience God's peace and freedom, we must be changed in heart and mind. For this to happen, we must do what Paul teaches in the verse quoted at the opening of this chapter:

> Finally, brothers, whatever things are true, whatever things are honest, whatever things are just, whatever things are pure, whatever things are lovely, whatever things are of good report, if there is any virtue, and if there is any praise, think on these things.
>
> —PHILIPPIANS 4:8, MEV

The Greek word used for *think* in this verse is *logizomai*. It implies concentrated, focused effort. Paul is telling us that we must intentionally fix our minds on those things that reflect the truth of who God is and what He thinks about us, His dearly loved children.

This means we are to think on whatever is reliable and honest. We must direct our attention to the noble, or those things that are worthy of respect. We are to meditate on what is righteous—that which conforms to God's standards and which merits approval. We need to uphold all that is pure, or those things that are moral and chaste. We are called to see the lovely—all that is pleasing and agreeable— and to behold what is admirable and worthy of praise.

The following quote by Ralph Waldo Emerson creates a

profound picture of what can develop in our lives as a result of what we choose to think on:

> Sow a thought, reap an action.
> Sow an action, reap a habit.
> Sow a habit, reap a character.
> Sow a character, reap a destiny![1]

The prophet Isaiah tells us how to prepare our minds to sow right thoughts: "You will guard him and keep him in perfect and constant peace whose mind [both its inclination and its character] is stayed on You, because he commits himself to You, leans on You, and hopes confidently in You" (Isa. 26:3, AMP). When we set our minds on good things, on the truth of God's Word, and on God Himself, we will experience perfect peace. Not only that, but we will be strengthened to walk according to God's Word in our full identity as sons and daughters of God, no matter how many obstacles are set in our way.

Let's agree now that we will choose to set our minds on God and thus begin to sow thoughts that lead to righteous actions, to sow actions that exhibit a holy lifestyle, to sow habits that build virtuous character, and to sow character that will empower kingdom destiny.

THINK ON THESE THINGS

So how exactly do we begin to think on good things? The apostle Paul gave us clear instructions in Philippians 4. As we apply his counsel, we will find ourselves walking victoriously in Christ. Let's look at each item in Paul's list in Philippians 4:8 so our thought life can be transformed and, as a result, we can experience amazing peace and freedom.

Whatsoever is true

The Greek word for *true* is *athletes*, which means "real, truthful, honest, and having integrity." The problem is, many of us do not focus on things that are true, real, and honest but on things that worry and concern us. A study done by Dr. Walter Calvert and funded by the National Science Foundation revealed some startling statistics about human beings and worry. Here's what he found[2]:

- Thirty percent of our worries are about events in the past

- Forty percent of the things we worry about never happen

- Twelve percent of our worries are unfounded health concerns

- Ten percent of our worries are over minor and trivial issues

- *Only 8 percent* of our worries are over real, legitimate issues (emphasis mine)

What can we learn from this study? As stated in previous chapters, Satan first and foremost is a liar: "He was a murderer from the beginning, not holding to the truth, for there is no truth in him. When he lies, he speaks his native language, for he is a liar and the father of lies" (John 8:44). Therefore, we have to determine not to accept condemning thoughts or lies from the devil—the accuser of the brethren—which cause us to fret about things that we cannot change. We must determine not to worry about the past—it's over—and we must resolve not to agonize over the future.

Instead, we must purpose to focus on God's truth, which will empower us daily in our spiritual walk and in life. It is by the truth, which is the Word of God, that we are sanctified (purified, consecrated, separated unto the Lord, and made holy). (See John 17:17, AMP.) So if we are going to train our minds to think on what is good, we must fill ourselves with God's truth.

This is one reason it is so important to memorize God's Word. I strongly encourage you to make this a practice. It may seem complicated, but it's not so daunting. Begin by inviting the Holy Spirit to cause His Word to come alive in you, in your thoughts, and in your emotions. Ask Him to anoint the words so they become a part of your new identity in Christ. Allow God to direct you to scriptures that speak to you personally, and then highlight and memorize them.

When I memorize Scripture, I write the verses God points out to me on note cards and hang them in places where I will see them on a regular basis—the bathroom mirror, the refrigerator, the microwave. I include portions of these verses on the home screen of my cell phone and on the screensaver of my personal computer. Then I read or recite them out loud.

As you commit to thinking on things that are true, consider memorizing the following verses, which highlight the source of all truth:

> I am the true vine, and My Father is the vinedresser.
> —JOHN 15:1, MEV

> And we know that the Son of God has come and has given us understanding, so that we may know Him who is true, and we are in Him who is true—His Son Jesus Christ. He is the true God and eternal life
> —1 JOHN 5:20, MEV

Whatsoever is honorable

The Greek word for *honorable* is *semnos*. It means "to be venerated or worthy of respect as a result of upstanding character." It also signifies being dignified. In other words, we are to be people of honor, character, and dignity—and that begins with our thought life. Many things are not respectable, and as Christians you and I should not think about or dwell on those things. This does not mean that we hide our heads in the sand and avoid or choose to be ignorant of what is unpleasant and displeasing in the world around us. Ignorance is not bliss. Rather, as sons and daughters of our heavenly Father, we are to be the reflection of Him and His kingdom in this dark world. And this means that we must not focus our attention on dishonorable things and permit them to control our thoughts.

How do we think on what is honorable? We choose to live a lifestyle of honor. We learn to honor those with whom we are in relationship. If we have treated anyone dishonorably, we now choose to act respectfully toward him or her. If we have been steeped in entertainment that dishonors our faith, now is the time for us to repent and stop. We choose to honor ourselves and God by living a life of integrity that reflects the beauty and privilege of our Christian faith.

To aid in this process, I recommend memorizing the following key scriptures:

> The Father…has committed all judgment to the Son, that all men should honor the Son, just as they honor the Father.
> —JOHN 5:22—23, MEV

> The wise inherit honor.
> —PROVERBS 3:35

> The LORD God of Israel says…"Those who honor Me, I will honor."
> —1 SAMUEL 2:30, MEV

Whatsoever is just

The Greek word for *just* is *dikaios*. It is translated "righteous, innocent, faultless, guiltless." A just person is one who learns to think on what God approves of and accepts. This person is used of God, and his or her way of thinking, feeling, and acting is conformed to the will of God. Just individuals relate to all people from a place of kingdom love and authority. This means we always respond to people from the Father's heart of love while also speaking His truth, wisdom, and righteousness without compromise.

Allow me to explain further. We have ministered to numerous individuals who were trapped in the deception of homosexuality, addiction to pornography or drugs, or involved in any number of other sinful lifestyles. One of the most important ways we model the Father's heart of love is by stating up front that we will love those whom God sends to us, but in no way will we compromise the truth of Scripture. It is our model to speak the truth in love and while expressing love, to identify the lies of the enemy— strongholds of the mind—and render them broken in the name of Jesus. And where it is necessary, we must challenge these individuals to take responsibility for their wrong and sinful choices, repent, and commit to walk out their freedom by submitting themselves to spiritual accountability and choosing a godly lifestyle.

We walk in God's wisdom and authority in order to pass judgment (exercise our judicial authority in Christ) against the schemes of the enemy that are targeting our thoughts and emotions so that we can be set free and see our brothers and sisters in the Lord delivered.

An action step that we can take personally in passing judgment against the strongholds of the enemy is to begin to declare out loud that his lies no longer have a right to access our thought lives. We must determine that enough is enough and no longer be timid to speak boldly (out loud!) that these strongholds of the mind and emotions have no right to torment us!

Keeping in mind the following scriptures can help us as we learn to think on what is just and live out true justice:

> Your Kingdom, O God, will last forever and ever; its commands are always just and right.
>
> —Hebrews 1:8, tlb

> I will sing of mercy and justice; to You, O Lord, I will sing.
>
> —Psalm 101:1, mev

> The Lord executes righteousness and justice [not for me only, but] for all who are oppressed.
>
> —Psalm 103:6, amp

Whatsoever is pure

The Greek word for *pure* is *hagnos*. It means "innocent, venerable, sacred, and pure from carnality." What is carnality? In our culture we are constantly bombarded with materials glorifying impurity, sexual sin, and darkness. We are to think on what is chaste, modest, and morally pure. As believers, we must focus on gracious and righteous thoughts, not on the carnal thoughts encouraged by this corrupt world. It is our privilege to set the standard of a pure life to the world around us.

Let us remember these scriptures as we joyfully let our lives reflect purity:

> Blessed are the pure in heart, for they shall see God.
>
> —Matthew 5:8, mev

> Create in me a pure heart, O God, and renew a right spirit within me.
>
> —Psalm 51:10, mev

Whatsoever is lovely

The Greek word for *lovely* is *prosphiles*. It signifies something that is "acceptable, pleasing, agreeable, beautiful, and attractive," and speaks of that which promotes peace rather than conflict. In a world in which conflict is ever-present, thinking on what is lovely can be an incredibly difficult task to accomplish. However, we can choose to see the loveliness of the Lord and His magnificent work in His creation of those around us and this world. We can be the voice of truth and the example that guides those around us to redirect their focus to things that are lovely.

To walk this out we must learn to love all people with the heart of God, even those we would consider unlovely. We must love all people, no matter their race, ethnicity, or beliefs, and follow the model Jesus set by reaching beyond our religious thinking to minister to the lost world. We are to grow to such a place in our walk with the Lord that the Holy Spirit will give us great wisdom in difficult situations, thus allowing us to exemplify the love and wisdom of our Lord.

The following truths will guide us in focusing on what is lovely:

> How lovely is Your dwelling place, O LORD of Hosts!
> My soul longs, yes, even faints for the courts of the
> LORD; my heart and my body cry out for the living God.
> —PSALM 84:1–2, MEV

> The earth is full of the lovingkindness of the LORD.
> —PSALM 33:5, MEV

Whatsoever is of good report

The Greek word for *good report* is *euphemos*. It relates to what is positive and constructive rather than negative and destructive. Simply put, things that are of good report are the things that are worth talking about—and thus thinking about.

Most people are familiar with the saying that there are two types of people—those who see the glass half empty, and those who see the glass half full. We can choose to be people who believe the good report and see the glass half full. How do we do this? By learning to find what is good and positive in circumstances. Begin to discipline yourself not to linger on the negatives. Learn to think before you speak, and let the goodness of God and His report be your focus.

As we determine to think on whatsoever is of good report, let us keep the following verses in mind:

> We know that God causes all things to work together for good to those who love God, to those who are called according to His purpose.
> —ROMANS 8:28, NAS

> Praise the LORD, my soul, and forget not all his benefits…who satisfies your desires with good things.
> —PSALM 103:2, 5

If there be any virtue

If something has *virtue,* it will motivate us to do better in every area of our life. The Greek word for *virtue* used in this verse is *arete.* It means "wonderful, manifestation of power and excellence." As Christians, we cannot afford to waste mind power or emotional strength on thoughts that would tear us or others down if they were shared. We must choose instead to model excellence.

What are some practical examples of how we would do this? Be the employee at work who exemplifies a spirit of excellence. Show up on time. Promote unity in your church, home, family, and workplace. Be a good steward of the things God has entrusted to you, and train your thoughts to think on the following promises:

> Those who have served well gain an excellent standing and great assurance in their faith in Christ Jesus.
> —1 TIMOTHY 3:13

> Those who have believed in God might be careful to maintain good works. These things are good and profitable to everyone.
> —TITUS 3:8, MEV

If there be any praise

If something is deserving of praise, it is worth commending to ourselves and to others. *Epainos,* the Greek word for *praiseworthy,* means "to give our praise to what is worthy of commendation and fame." I know of no one more deserving of praise, fame, and commendation than our heavenly Father, magnificent Savior, and consuming Holy Spirit.

Set your praise on Him. Choose to audibly praise and thank Him for the things He has done for you or revealed to you. Thank and praise Him in advance for the things for which you are still awaiting a spiritual breakthrough. Consider the following verses as you make praising God a natural part of your lifestyle:

> Let my soul live and praise You, and let Your judgments come to my aid.
> —PSALM 119:175, MEV

> To Him who sits on the throne and to the Lamb be blessing and honor and glory and power, forever and ever!
> —REVELATION 5:13, MEV

THE POWER OF AFFIRMATION

Now that we understand what things we are to think on, we must learn to put this model into practice. David writes in Psalm 119:38–40, "Affirm your promises to me—promises made to all who fear you. Deflect the harsh words of my critics—but what you say is always so good. See how hungry I am for your counsel; preserve my life through your righteous ways!" (THE MESSAGE). The Greek word for *affirm* in this verse is *bebaioo.* It means "to cause something to be known as certain, increase in inner strength, and implying greater firmness of character." It also means "the assertion that something exists or is true, a statement or proposition that is declared to be true."

As we read and meditate on the Scriptures, our heavenly Father affirms His Word to us, confirming its truth to our hearts. As He does so, He affirms *us* as well with His words, His love, and His presence. When He affirms us, we are filled with strength and gain the resolve to follow Him.

Sadly, however, too often we sabotage God's affirming words with our own negative self-talk. In chapter 9 we discussed how many words people speak and the average number of thoughts that go through our minds each day. We may not always realize it, but we also speak to ourselves in these thoughts. As we previously discussed, as much as 80 percent of our thoughts contains negative content. However, the most exceptional professional athletes are said to have learned how to practice positive and affirming self-talk in order to perform well and win their games. The late Dorothy Harris, PhD, who was a professor of sport psychology at Pennsylvania State University, said, "The only difference between the best performance and the worst performance is the variation in our self-talk and the self-thoughts and attitudes we carry around with us."[3] Dr. Harris's words can be applied not only to sports but also to life in general.

Focused positive thinking and self-talk are vital if we want to walk in victory. Our belief systems are built on what we think and on what we say to ourselves and not just on what we say out loud. This explains why the words of our mouths (what we speak to others), the meditations of our hearts (what we speak to ourselves), and the words of others (those to whom we listen), whether positive or negative, significantly establish what we think, what we do, and who we will eventually become. If we want to think on things that are good, our self-talk should be pleasing to God and in agreement with His Word. Doing this will affirm and strengthen us.

FOCUSING ON OUR KINGDOM IDENTITY

When we think on what is good, one of the results is that God affirms and instills within our thoughts and emotions what I call "kingdom identities." These are beliefs, decisions, attitudes, expectations, and vows that agree with what God says in His Word about our identity in Him. Paul lays this truth out for us in 2 Corinthians 1:20–22:

> Whatever God has promised gets stamped with the Yes of Jesus. In him, this is what we preach and pray, the great Amen, God's Yes and our Yes together, gloriously evident. God affirms us, making us a sure thing in Christ, putting his Yes within us. By his Spirit he has stamped us with his eternal pledge—a sure beginning of what he is destined to complete.
>
> —THE MESSAGE

In order to fill our minds with kingdom identities, we need to continue to take practical steps. Make time to pull away and spend time with the Lord, seeking His Word for what He says about you. Invite the Holy Spirit to guide you. Begin to make a list of the scripture promises the Lord highlights to you that focus on your identity in Him. Then make it a regular practice to read and declare aloud the inherited promises that are yours as God's beloved child. The following promises from Scripture will help you get started:

- I can do everything through Him who gives me strength (Phil. 4:13).

- God is able to make all grace abound to me (2 Cor. 9:8).

- I am accepted by Christ (Rom. 15:7).

- I am alive with Christ (Gal. 2:20).

- I hunger and thirst after righteousness; therefore I will be filled (Matt. 5:6).

- The anointing I receive from God remains in me (1 John 2:27).

- I am Christ's ambassador (2 Cor. 5:20).

- I am adopted; I am a child of the heavenly Father (Gal. 4:5–7).

- I am Christ's bride adorned in jewels, clothed in garments of salvation, and arrayed in a robe of righteousness (Isa. 61:10).

- I am an heir of God and a coheir with Christ (Gal. 3:29; 8:17).

- I am being conformed to the image of Christ (Rom. 8:29).

- I am becoming mature and attaining to the whole measure of the fullness of Christ (Eph. 4:13).

- I have been given to and belong to Christ (John 17:9).

- I am chosen; I am part of a royal priesthood and a holy nation; I belong to God (1 Pet. 2:9).

- I have been called out of darkness into God's marvelous light (1 Pet. 2:9).

- I am blessed with every spiritual blessing in Christ (Eph. 1:3).

- Christ is my life (Col. 3:4).

- I am clothed in Christ (Gal. 3:27).

- I am free (Rom. 8:2).

- I am a friend of God (John 15:14–15).

- I lack no wisdom (James 1:5).

- I do not have a spirit of fear, but rather I have power, love, and a sound mind (2 Tim. 1:7).

- I am not condemned, because I am in Christ Jesus (Rom. 8:1).

- I have the mind of Christ (1 Cor. 2:16).

- I am favored (Ps. 5:12).

- I am God's handiwork (Eph. 2:10).

- God will never forsake me (Heb. 13:5).

- I am yielded to God (Rom. 6:13).

- I have victory through Jesus Christ (1 Cor. 15:57).

- I am precious, honored in God's sight, and loved (Isa. 43:4).

THE POWER OF TESTIMONY

There is power in knowing our kingdom identity, and there is also power in sharing our testimony. When we remember the miraculous things God has done in our lives, we are further encouraged and our faith in our kingdom identity (who God has created us to be) is increased. For me personally, when I share where I have come from and where the Lord has brought me, my faith is greatly increased. And that causes me to stand and believe that His miraculous hand will continue to move on my behalf.

Allow me to ask a few questions: When was the last time God moved in your life in such a powerful way that you could not deny His miraculous hand in your circumstances? Do you see God's miracles in your life on a regular basis? What are you believing God for right now? Take time to recall the miraculous encounters that have occurred in your life, and let them stir your faith. If you are not currently pressing in for God to move miraculously in your life, make a list of the areas in which you need God's supernatural hand to move. Pray over these areas and seek Him for divine intervention.

One final question: do the previous questions make you uncomfortable? Let me explain why I ask. Many believers I meet do not realize that they can ask for personal encounters and blessings from God. Some wonder if they should. I believe that because you are reading this book, you desire to walk in a life of freedom and victory, and to have a mind filled with God's perfect peace. I believe that you share my desire to reach for a life that is set apart and honorable to God—a life that desires God's best and is marked by His richest kingdom blessings. If you want to receive all that God has for you, you must realize that God wants to pour out His love on you and cause His anointing, presence, grace, truth, love, and power to surround you and enable you to live out your kingdom identity in a powerful and beautiful way.

Some of us are hesitant to be bold in our prayer life and to trust God's faithfulness. We ask Him just for enough. But friends, God wants us to abandon ourselves in His love and grace and trust that He is more than willing to bless us and fill us to overflowing. The beauty is that when we do this, God's great plan for us will enfold us and sweep us forward into the profoundly significant and joyous life He has destined for us.

I am not saying that when we do this, everything in life will be perfect. We will experience times of trial. But when we abandon ourselves to God's mighty love and grace, the Lord will deepen our trust in Him and empower us to believe His good report and the truth that "God causes all things to work together for good to those who love God" (Rom. 8:28,

NAS). As we focus our thoughts on what is good and right and true and just, God can bring us to a place of peace so that no matter what circumstances we face, we can be deeply satisfied in knowing that we are in God's plan.

JABEZ—A LIFE BEYOND THE LIMITS

A man in the Old Testament who had a negative start in life discovered this powerful truth. First Chronicles 4:9–10, the only two verses in the Bible that talk about this man named Jabez, tells us his story of victory:

> Now Jabez was more honorable than his brothers, and his mother called his name Jabez, saying, "Because I bore him in hardship." Then Jabez called on the God of Israel, saying, "Oh, that You would indeed bless me and enlarge my territory, that Your hand might be with me, and that You would keep mefrom evil, that it may not bring me hardship!" So God granted what he asked.
>
> —MEV

Who is this man who prayed in such faith and was blessed by God? From what we can tell, Jabez lived in southern Israel sometime after the conquest of Canaan. He was born into the tribe of Judah and eventually became the notable head of a clan. Some believe that the city of Jabez, mentioned in 1 Chronicles 2:55, is named after him. If this is the case, then in history the Jews speak of Jabez as a famous doctor of the law who had many disciples who followed him. It seems, too, by the abrupt mention of Jabez in 1 Chronicles that his name was well known when Ezra wrote this book of the Bible.

Let's look at his name, because this is really where the story of Jabez begins. His mother gave him the Hebrew name *Yabets*, meaning "to grieve, sorrow, or pain." Why would a mother name her child this? To be honest, it is hard for me to fathom. Maybe she experienced a traumatic pregnancy or an exceptionally difficult delivery. Perhaps her family was in a financially difficult place, and the thought of another child brought them anxiety. It is possible that the name reflects sorrowful conditions surrounding the tribe of Judah at the time. Whatever the reason, it was not a great thing for a child to be given a name that proclaimed pain and sorrow every time it was spoken.

To compound the issue, the name Jabez really did not give this child much hope for the future. In Jewish culture names were often given to predict someone's potential. In a sense, a name was considered to be a prophetic word concerning the identity and destiny of an individual. This raises even more questions as to why a mother would mark her son with such a name, considering the sorrowful future it could bring him. However, Jabez himself determined to seek an authority higher than the person who gave him his name.

Despite the negative outcome his name should have brought, Jabez chose to think on and live out what was good. As a result, he is recorded in history as an honorable man before God. I believe Jabez knew his only hope for overcoming the stigma of his name was to fervently put his hope in the God of new beginnings. His devotion to the Lord is unmistakable in his cry to God: "Oh, that you would bless me and enlarge my territory! Let your hand be with me, and keep me from harm so that I will be free from pain" (1 Chron. 4:10).

Remember, as we discussed in chapter 8, that to bless in the biblical sense means to ask for or to impart supernatural favor. When we pray for the blessing of God, we are not asking for more of what we can get for ourselves such as a Porsche, a mansion, or a six-figure income. God might choose to give us great financial blessing through a creative kingdom idea that He imparts to us as a result of prayer. But in this instance, Jabez was crying out for the wonderful, never-ending goodness that only God has the power to know about or give. Jabez was totally committing himself to God and therefore wanted for himself nothing more or less than what God wanted for him.

Jabez wanted to become wholly immersed in what God was doing in him, through him, and around him. And friends, God answered the prayer of Jabez. He blessed him, enlarged his territory, protected him, and kept him from pain and evil. If God can do this for Jabez, He can do it for you and me. When we live honorable and wholly committed lives before our Lord; focus on what is good; and ask God to bless, enlarge, and protect us, we position ourselves to become recipients of our Father's unending blessings. What does it mean to pray in agreement with God for yourself? It means to pray what He wants in your life.

THE BLESSING THAT ROCKED MY WORLD

Sometimes, even when we know what is true and right and that we are to think on those things, our thoughts become weighed down with distractions, hurts, or discouragement. During a particular season in my life when my heart was burdened with grief, I needed a reminder of what is true. I had my own Jabez moment when my eyes were opened afresh to the truth of my kingdom identity and to what God says about me.

I have been blessed with supportive, loving parents. I am very close to my mother and love her dearly. However, throughout my life I have always been a daddy's girl, and I just loved being with my dad. Whether we were target shooting, watching old movies such as *White Christmas*, going fishing, attending a cattle auction, or sitting on the forty-yard line of a Dallas Cowboys game, I just enjoyed my dad's presence. I still love him with all my heart and miss him dearly.

The week before my father's passing, my mom, my sister,

and I were with him at the hospital. Someone was always by his side, even throughout the night. One night I stayed with him by myself. It had been a long, difficult night due to the fact that my father was unable to sleep. Even so, he never complained one time. In the early morning I thought he had finally drifted off to sleep, so I quietly went over to the vanity to brush my teeth and comb my hair before the doctors came by for their early morning rounds. As I stood before the mirror, my father in his loving voice called my name from his bed. "Becca?"

"Oh, Daddy," I replied, "I am sorry I woke you."

"You did not wake me. I was not asleep, just resting my eyes," he told me. "I want to tell you something. You are such a beautiful woman. I am so proud of you, and I love you so much." Tears rolled down my cheeks as my father shared his totally abandoned, genuine love toward me.

I walked over to his bed, held his hand, and lovingly replied, "I love you too, Daddy. So much. I love that you're my dad." Later that day, as I read the Bible to him, he smiled and looked at me and said, "Don't you ever stop reading and teaching the Word of God." Those moments are so beautiful to me, because they were my father's way of giving me his blessing.

Not only did my dad speak his blessing, but he also expressed his love to me in a very special way. For as long as I can remember, one of my dad's favorite ways to express affection to me was to gently tap my nose three times while smiling his familiar smile of approval and love. I loved it when my dad did this.

The day my father passed away was a surprise to us. We knew he was sick, but that particular morning he had been doing exceptionally well, and the doctors had given him a good report. As I stood by his bed after the physicians' morning rounds, my dad looked at me and smiled that wonderful father's smile, and raised his finger and gently tapped my nose three times. Seven hours later we stood by my father's bedside as the presence of angels and our Lord filled that hospital room, and my dad slipped into eternity.

While we rejoiced that he was now with the Lord, I was heartbroken to be without my dad. No more fishing together, shooting guns together, working jigsaw puzzles together, or having old movie night with him and my girls. No more being in his presence, which brought me safety, peace, love, and joy. But most of all, as I told the Lord as I cried myself to sleep that night, "I am so going to miss the love taps on my nose. I so loved that gesture of affection from my father."

Three weeks after my father's funeral, I attended a leadership meeting. Because of the loss I had just suffered and an upcoming leadership trip to Spain I was scheduled to make, my friends gathered around me to minister to me. I closed my eyes to receive. While standing in the presence of the Lord, I suddenly felt three love taps on my nose in the exact rhythm my dad used to use. Startled, I gasped and quickly opened my eyes to see who was in front of me. There stood one of my dearest friends, Tommi Femrite.

Surprised by my response, she lovingly looked at me and smiled just as my father used to smile. Then she explained, "Becca, I don't understand why, but the Lord told me to tap you three times on the nose, and when you opened your eyes, I was to look at you and smile, and it was to be a smile of approval and love." I instantly began to weep, and I shared with Tommi about how my dad used to tap my nose and smile to show me his love and affection.

"Tommi, on the night my father passed away, I told the Lord that I was so going to miss those love taps from my dad."

Her response to me was, "Well, God had me here tonight to make sure that you received those love taps. Becca, He loves you so much, and He wants you to know that when you need those taps of love, He can and will bring them to you." She then asked, "Becca, do you know the prophetic meaning of those three love taps on your nose?"

Puzzled by her question, I said, "No, I don't. Is there a prophetic meaning?"

"Yes, I actually did a recent study and teaching on this. When the children of Israel were preparing to go into battle, each of them chose the warhorse he would ride into battle with other nations. When the warrior found the horse that he wanted to ride into battle, he would designate his choice by tapping that horse on the nose. Becca, I believe the Lord wants you to know that through that touch of affection from your father, even if your dad did not realize it, he was actually prophesying your calling and destiny to the nations of the world."

I was stunned and moved to tears at the incredible goodness of our God. I travel the nations each year, and to date I have traveled internationally more than fifty times. In my place of loss, the Lord sent a prophet to me to tap me on my nose exactly the way my father did and to explain the prophetic meaning of this expression of love.

Friends, our God can and will rock our worlds with His amazing goodness and faithfulness. If He can affirm me by sending a prophet to tap me on my nose to bring assurance and peace to my heart, He can affirm you too. As you turn your thoughts to things that are true, honorable, just, pure, lovely, of good report, and praiseworthy, God will show you your identity in Him and bring you what you need to experience His glorious freedom and victory in your life.

Let's Pray in Agreement With the Goodness of God

Lord, David prayed in Psalm 19:7–9 that Your words are perfect and right and radiant and bring joy to the heart. I pray in agreement with him and choose to think on, believe in, and receive Your goodness that is revealed to us in Your Word. The revelation of You, God, is whole and is able to pull my life together. Lord, Your signposts are clear, and they point out the right road for me to follow. The life maps You lay out before me are right, and they show me the way to joy. Your directions are plain and easy to see. Your reputation, God, is as twenty-four-carat gold with a lifetime guarantee.

Lord, I thank You for Your blessings, and I ask You to bless me so that I can walk out a life of honor and blessing with an enlarged territory and with Your hand of protection keeping evil from me. Give me built-in Holy Spirit radar to detect wrong thoughts within me, and grant me Your great peace and favor as I commit this day to think on what is good, honorable, true, just, pure, lovely, of good report, full of virtue and praise, and in line with my kingdom identity and destiny. Thank You, Lord. I love You. In Jesus's name, amen.

Chapter 11

BUT WE HAVE THE
MIND OF CHRIST

*Who has known or understood the mind (the counsels and
purposes) of the Lord so as to guide and instruct Him and
give Him knowledge? But we have the mind of Christ.*

[1 Corinthians 2:16, AMP]

I T IS AN amazing thing to say that we as believers possess the very mind of Jesus! To some it may sound vain
or distant, or be difficult to comprehend that we can
know God's mind. How can we, in our imperfect human
state, begin to think like Him? How can we learn to walk in
such a close relationship with Him that we know His mind
and understand the purposes of His heart?

The reality is we are all in process. The process of understanding the mind of God is a critical journey to complete,
but God has given us the Holy Spirit, the Bible, His love, His
presence, and His truth to help us grow in spiritual wisdom,
depth, and maturity. We read in 1 Corinthians 2:16:

> Who has known or understood the mind (the coun-
> sels and purposes) of the Lord so as to guide and
> instruct Him and give Him knowledge? But we have
> the mind of Christ (the Messiah) and do hold the
> thoughts (feelings and purposes) of His heart.
>
> —AMP

The Greek word for *know* in this verse is *ginosko*. It
means "to understand, perceive and identify with as in
intimacy between a husband and wife." Friends, that is

pretty intimate. This is how well we are to know the mind of the Lord.

At the time of this writing, my husband and I have been married for twenty-five years. We know each other very well. If we are standing in a crowded room, I can glance at Greg and know what he is thinking based on the expression on his face, how he is engaged in a conversation, or how he is interacting with others. I know Greg, and he knows me. We know each other more intimately than anyone else knows either of us.

I realize that the depths of our Redeemer are unending, and this is the beauty of God's promise to give us the mind of Christ. We have the privilege of seeking Jesus, getting to know Him intimately, and learning to think on things that are pleasing to Him. As we pursue God in this way, we will encounter increasingly deeper depths of revelation and of His presence.

When each word in the phrase "to have the mind of Christ" is translated, the words mean to be so closely joined to a person or thing, as in a marriage or friendship, that we possess the same intellectual understanding, capacity for spiritual truth and ability to perceive divine things and to recognize goodness and hate evil. The phrase expresses that we have the power to consider and judge soberly, calmly, and impartially. It also means to think on and to know the thoughts, feelings, desires, and purposes of God.

I do not want to suggest in any way that we ourselves become "little gods." Absolutely not. Yet for those of us who are believers, seeking the mind of Christ does not mean reaching for something outside of ourselves, but rather discovering a kingdom inheritance that has been deposited within us.

Every time I have an encounter with Jesus, He unveils a new aspect of Himself to me. This is what He desires for all of us. He wants us to mature to such a place in our spiritual relationship with Him that we begin to experience His heart and we allow ourselves to receive more of His love. He wants us to walk in freedom and victory over strongholds. When we do, He can then entrust to us deeper revelations of His truth and purposes.

So what is Jesus's mind? What will we experience in increasing measure as we draw closer and closer to Christ? Let's take a look at several effects of drawing closer to God to know the mind of Christ.

WE WILL LOVE AS JESUS LOVES

Jesus is loving. The closer we draw to Him, the more we experience His immense love. We will not only encounter His love for us personally, but if we will ask for it, He will release an impartation of His love for everyone and everything He created, and our hearts will be consumed in ways we never thought possible.

Jesus loves the lost. He loves the poor. He loves the orphaned. He loves the widows. He loves His precepts. He loves creation. He loves children. He loves family. He loves the church, His bride. He loves His Father. He loves the Holy Spirit. He loves the Word of God. He loves the nations. He loves to be creative. He loves to bless. He loves, and is full of, compassion. He loves you. He loves me. The closer we get to Him, the more we will love what He loves.

We will never be as content as when we are conforming to, loving, and doing that which is pleasing to God. The more delight we take in fellowshipping and partnering with God, the nearer we come to the freedom, influence, and love for which we aim in our Christian walk. David shows us the way as he prays: "I will delight myself in Your commandments, which I love. My hands also will I lift up [in fervent supplication] to Your commandments, which I love, and I will meditate on Your statutes" (Ps. 119:47–48, AMP). When we commit to obeying God's commands and exert all the strength we have to carry them out, when we delight in them and genuinely love them, we will experience higher heights and deeper depths of God's unconditional love.

WE WILL KNOW AND LIVE IN THE TRUTH

If we want to avoid being deceived by the enemy, demonic strongholds, and the ways of this world, we have to know God's truth. Not only do we need to know the truth, but we are to be intimate with the truth. That means we must be intimate with Jesus, because to be intimate with Jesus is to be intimate with the truth. Jesus said concerning Himself, "I am the way and the truth and the life. No one comes to the Father except through me" (John 14:6). There is no deceit to be found within the person of our Redeemer.

The degree to which we know the Father's truth is the degree to which we will walk in freedom. We have discussed in depth the Father's heart of love for each of us. Love is vital, but it is His love and truth together that will position us to function as His church, the "pillar and foundation of the truth" (1 Tim. 3:15).

WE WILL STEP INTO CHRIST'S REDEMPTIVE PLAN AND PURPOSE

The better we know the mind of Christ, the more we will know of His redemptive plan and purpose. Many of us are familiar with the scripture, "If people can't see what God is doing, they stumble all over themselves; but when they attend to what he reveals, they are most blessed" (Prov. 29:18, THE MESSAGE). I believe that many people walk through life bound by strongholds, frustrated, and discontent because they never discover God's perfect plan for their lives. They live day to day with no hope, joy, or purpose.

Therefore, they give the enemy an open door to tell them harassing lies that their hopes will never come to pass and that they are unworthy of realizing their dreams. Countless individuals have passed into eternity without ever realizing their full kingdom potential.

So how do we know God's redemptive plan and purpose? Jesus instructs us, "Seek first his kingdom and his righteousness, and all these things will be given to you as well" (Matt. 6:33). The word *seek* suggests being continually in search of something or making a strenuous and diligent effort to obtain something. This is the intensity with which we should seek God's rule and power to be made manifest in our lives. Through the Holy Spirit we seek to obey Jesus's commands, possess His righteousness, remain separate from the world, and show Christ's love to everyone.

When this is our greatest desire, we will naturally wish to be obedient to God's will. We then will be empowered to receive His strategies and to fulfill His purposes. It is through seeking His kingdom that every spiritual blessing will come to us.

WE WILL WALK IN HOLINESS

Our Lord is a God of no compromise, and we too must refuse to compromise with the world, the flesh, and the devil. Jesus walked this earth as a man and was able to withstand every temptation Satan brought to Him. He was holy—without sin. Many messages preached today speak of our walking in holiness out of duty, and I absolutely agree with this, but I also teach that we have to *choose* a lifestyle of holiness. If we do not intentionally choose to live holy, then we will not experience this lifestyle and its benefits.

God is calling for a sold-out holiness movement birthed from individuals encountering the Father in all of His glory. When we encounter the Father's light and truth, and the fire of His magnificent holiness, He captivates our minds and hearts. Then we begin to desire to walk in purity and without compromise, because we have a deepened understanding of the power of His sacrifice on the cross, His resurrection life, and His great holiness. In this way we are empowered "to put on the new self, created to be like God in true righteousness and holiness" (Eph. 4:24).

WE WILL GROW IN HUMILITY

The Bible declares to us, "Let this mind be in you, which was also in Christ Jesus" (Phil. 2:5, MEV). What does this mind refer to? It refers to Jesus's willingness to humble Himself (Phil. 2:8).

Humility has many parallels to holiness. Andrew Murray so closely associated these two qualities that he wrote, "The great test of whether the holiness we profess to seek or to attain is truth and life will be *whether it produces an increasing humility in us*" (emphasis added).[1]

Humility does not imply that we are inferior. Humility is living confidently true to who God had called us to be without pride. Pride and confidence are not synonymous. We can be totally humble and yet have great confidence in our Lord. Humility exemplifies a preference for others, personal holiness, a lifestyle of obedience, and reverence of a holy God. A humble person is one who has a heart to serve and honor others and who does not boast pridefully. Humility believes in the promise that God exalts those who humble themselves before Him.

To understand what it means to have this mind-set that Jesus modeled, it is best to study the words of Jesus Himself. The following are key verses in which Jesus taught about humility:

Blessed are the poor in spirit, for theirs is the kingdom of heaven. Blessed are those who mourn, for they shall be comforted. Blessed are the meek, for they shall inherit the earth.

—MATTHEW 5:3–5, MEV

Take My yoke upon you, and learn from Me. For I am meek and lowly in heart, and you will find rest for your souls.

—MATTHEW 11:29, MEV

Therefore whoever humbles himself like this little child is the greatest in the kingdom of heaven.

—MATTHEW 18:4, MEV

Whoever would be great among you, let him serve you, and whoever would be first among you, let him be your slave.

—MATTHEW 20:26–27, MEV

He who is greatest among you shall be your servant.

—MATTHEW 23:11, MEV

Everyone who exalt himself will be humbled, and he who humbles himself will be exalted.

—LUKE 18:14, MEV

If then, your Lord and Teacher, have washed your feet, you also ought to wash one another's feet.

—JOHN 13:14, MEV

Let him who is greatest among you be as the younger, and he who rules as he who serves.

—LUKE 22:26–27, MEV

God did not tell us to do something that is impossible for us to do. God is not a man that He would misrepresent or lie. I steadfastly trust that if Jesus tells us to humble ourselves, we can, in fact, be humble. This does not mean that we can be perfect. Nor does it mean that we have arrived and have nothing more to learn about humility. We might face roadblocks along the journey. But if we stay away from pride, insecurity (which is false humility), and works of the flesh, we are well on our way to being victorious in this area of our lives. God will grant us freedom over pride. And He will promote and bring blessing and favor to those who are truly humble before Him.

We Will Welcome the Daily Filling of the Holy Spirit

The Lord has not left us alone in our pursuit of the empowered lifestyle indicative of having the mind of Christ. We have the Holy Spirit to guide us. Jesus modeled the prayer for us to pray when we need to invite the Holy Spirit to keep us from temptation: "Lead us not into temptation, but deliver us from the evil one" (Matt. 6:13). We all have a sin nature, and we will still sin in our fallen human state, but when we pray this prayer daily and invite the Holy Spirit to keep us from temptation and from the evil one (Satan), our God will be faithful to show us the way. And when we do sin, He will quickly bring it to light. When He does, it is important that we promptly repent.

Not only does the Holy Spirit keep us from temptation and evil, but He can baptize us with His fire and supernatural anointing. Think about this. From the time of Pentecost and the baptism of the Holy Spirit as recorded in Acts 2, we witness Peter and the disciples supernaturally emboldened to live holy, humble, abandoned lives. They were anointed to speak truth, fearlessly witness, perform miracles, raise the dead, shake cities and nations for God's kingdom, cast out demons, and take authority over the schemes of the enemy. The transformation in their spiritual walk after they were baptized by fire into the Holy Spirit is undeniable. The Holy Spirit is available to us to mark our spiritual journey with supernatural experiences and to validate that we are believers in Jesus Christ.

The Holy Spirit will always draw us closer to Jesus and bring us into encounters with Him. Friends, I cannot emphasize enough the depths of spiritual understanding, freedom, victory, and kingdom power the Holy Spirit can lead us into in order for us to see strongholds defeated. Invite His presence to fill, guide, and to empower you daily. Learn to live a life abiding (being vitally joined) in His presence. You will then, with His help, be strengthened and given the hope and ability to walk in agreement with our Lord and His intentions.

We Will Do What the Father Is Doing

During His ministry while on earth, Jesus did what He saw the Father doing. It is in hearing the voice of the Lord and His direction that we too will be empowered to obediently execute the Father's purposes. Jesus told His disciples:

> My Father has worked [even] until now, [He has never ceased working; He is still working] and I, too, must be at [divine] work... I assure you, most solemnly I tell you, the Son is able to do nothing of Himself (of His own accord); but He is able to do only what He sees the Father doing, for whatever the Father does is what the Son does in the same way [in His turn].
> —John 5:17, 19, amp

It is necessary for us to grasp the idea that Jesus did not work independently of His Father. He understood that He could do nothing unless His Father was already doing it. We can see this example through human relationships. We have all seen sons who look and act like their fathers and daughters who look and act like their mothers. We often say in our household that Kendall, our oldest daughter, is me on steroids! While in appearance she favors both my husband and myself, in personality she is me magnified to the nth degree. She models what has been modeled to her. Jesus, however, was relaying the idea that His relationship with His Father was on a higher level than that of a natural parent-child relationship. While He was imitating His Father's actions, He was also working in agreement and perfect harmony with His Father.

Jesus knew His Father's intent and purpose completely and absolutely because it became His intent and purpose as well. In saying that He could do only what His Father did, Jesus gave a powerful message. He was actually stating that He had no plans that were differing, opposite of, or uncooperative with those of His Father. He had no selfish ambitions or motives of His own. He and His Father acted in complete accord in their natures, plans, purposes, and actions.

Jesus was fully God, but He was also fully man. Just like you and me, in His human nature He had to learn to walk in the fullness of His anointing and destiny. In order to do so, He had to pull away from the crowds, pray, seek the Father, and hear His voice. He set His mind and emotions on what God was revealing, and He advanced in His calling in unity with the plans of His Father. Therefore, Jesus lacked no confidence when tempted by the enemy and when taking authority over demonic schemes against others and Himself. Jesus and His Father worked together in restoring, reestablishing, and extending the kingdom of God. Jesus was a Son of action.

How does this apply to us? This is the model for us as sons and daughters of our heavenly Father. We too are to advance in permission, meaning that we do what we see the Father doing. When we walk in accordance with the guidance of the Holy Spirit, we, like Jesus, are able from this place to see the schemes of Satan defeated in our lives and to walk in our kingdom destiny.

WE WILL HATE WHAT JESUS HATES

The Word of God clearly shows how our Lord feels about Satan, his evil schemes, and sin's awfulness, and we are to share His mind-set in this matter. Consider the following passages:

> While there has never been any question about your honesty in these matters—I couldn't be more proud of you!—I want you also to be smart, making sure every "good" thing is the *real* thing. Don't be gullible in regard to smooth-talking evil. Stay alert like this, and before you know it the God of peace will come down on Satan with both feet, stomping him into the dirt. Enjoy the best of Jesus!
> —ROMANS 16:19–20, THE MESSAGE

> God will shatter the heads of His enemies.
> —PSALM 68:21, AMP

> May he judge and defend the poor of the people, deliver the children of the needy, and crush the oppressor.
> —PSALM 72:4, AMP

Friends, this is not love language! Our Savior obviously hates evil and likewise wants us to hate evil. Ask God to give you a righteous anger toward the enemy of our souls and his evil army.

WE WILL STAND FIRM AGAINST TEMPTATION

Jesus models for us how to respond to evil and to Satan's temptations. Before being fully released into His earthly ministry, Jesus faced the enemy's fiercest temptations. He had to successfully resist temptation, unlike Adam and Eve, who had failed. He also had to show us how to stand against

Satan's tricks intended to draw us into rebellion and sin. Thus, "Jesus was led by the Spirit into the wilderness to be tempted by the devil" (Matt. 4:1).

In the wilderness Jesus fasted and prayed for forty days and forty nights. It is sensible for us to conclude that Jesus spent this time in prayer, meditating on God's Word, and being filled with the Spirit in order to prepare for the work His Father had designed for Him to accomplish. At the end of the fasting period, Satan wasted no time in attempting to lure Jesus into rebellion. The Bible records three temptations Satan presented to the Lord, each with an underlying threat to Jesus's kingdom identity.

The first temptation—to acquire food by turning stones into bread—took advantage of Jesus's hunger: "The tempter came to him and said, 'If you are the Son of God, tell these stones to become bread'" (Matt. 4:3). Notice how Satan initiated this temptation: "If you are the Son of God." By using the word *if*, Satan was not questioning whether Jesus was the Son of God; he was challenging our Lord to prove that He was. Satan was essentially saying, "Since you are the Son of God, take this opportunity to show it by commanding that stones be turned into bread."

Jesus refused the devil's temptation by quoting from Scripture: "Man is not dependent on bread alone for life—God is the source of life" (Matt. 4:4; see also Deut. 8:3). We all know that Jesus came to restore mankind by offering us salvation. Therefore, the enemy slyly tempted our Savior with satisfying the desires of His flesh in an attempt to gain authority over Him.

After hearing Jesus quote the Word of God, Satan himself turned to Scripture, Psalm 91, in his second temptation. As seen in this confrontation, Satan and his army of darkness are fully able to quote Scripture. I have seen in my years of ministry that demonic strongholds are able to quote Bible verses better than many believers. Being the father of lies, however, Satan and his dark army will misuse and twist the intent of the verses in order to deceive, control, and confuse.

Satan led Jesus to the highest point of the Temple in an attempt to get Him to jump to the ground. In a taunting voice, he again challenged our Lord, saying, "If you really are the Son of God, then would You not be rescued by angels?" (Matt. 6:6). This temptation followed the pattern of seduction that led Adam and Eve into the Fall. Recall the enemy's words to Eve: "Did God really say...?" In this case Satan is saying, "Didn't God say...?" Yet Jesus was not fooled. He responded again by declaring wisdom and truth from the Word of God: "It is also written: Do not put the Lord your God to the test" (Matt. 4:7).

The Greek word for *test*, or *tempt*, in this verse is *ekpeiraseis*, which means "to test in order to see how far one can go or how much one can get away with." This temptation by the enemy was an attempt to interfere with Jesus's personal relationship with His Father. Jesus had been called to restore true worship to God under His Father's direction. Satan's ungodly demand here was that Jesus attempt to make God prove Himself, which would have demonstrated a lack of faith in the Father's guidance.

We must never allow Satan to draw us into a challenge to prove God's promises and faithfulness to us. God wants to impact and restore this lost world. He does not have to prove Himself to Satan. Satan has already been found guilty and has been cast out of heaven. We now get to help in his humiliation and defeat as we take authority over him in our lives, in Jesus's name.

In his third challenge Satan took Jesus to a high mountain and "showed Him all the kingdoms of the world and their splendor. 'All this I will give you,' he said, 'if you will bow down and worship me'" (Matt. 4:8). In coming to the earth,

Jesus was to defeat the enemy, restore mankind through God's plan of redemption, and establish His kingdom in our lives and on earth. Satan was making an outright play to usurp this divine agenda and become the one who would be worshipped.

Can you imagine the audacity of Satan to tempt Jesus into bowing and worshipping him, the father of all evil and deception? But in order to overcome and gain authority over Satan, Jesus in His humanness had to withstand the temptation. Our Lord authoritatively refused the offer and sharply rebuked him: "Away from me, Satan! For it is written: 'Worship the Lord your God, and serve him only'" (Matt. 4:10).

Jesus has walked where we have walked. He was tempted by Satan. However, He did not become a victim of the enemy's attacks. Instead, He used the opportunity to rise to the position of victor. We are to be like Him. Let me pose a question: Why do we put more faith and trust in the lies of the enemy than we do in the promises of God? We waste so much time and energy believing Satan's lies. To have the mind of Christ, we must choose to stand in God's truth against the deceptions, demonic challenges, and evil schemes of our foe. When you are tempted by the enemy, do as Jesus did. Do not succumb to the lies of the enemy, which can lead to rebellion. Instead, speak the Word of God in faith, and audibly rebuke Satan's demonic and taunting lies!

WE WILL NOT BE BOUND BY A RELIGIOUS SPIRIT

Jesus walked in total authority over sin, and we are to do the same. But one of the enemy's most deceptive and deadly attacks upon believers is to try to divert our attention from the cross of Jesus, which gives us victory over sin, to the evil in our lives. He knows we will become what we behold. (See 2 Corinthians 3:18.) This results in us having a religious spirit.

What is a religious spirit? It is a demonic spirit that seeks to substitute religious activity for the power of the Holy Spirit in our lives. As long as we keep looking at the deception in our lives and are overcome by our weaknesses and failures, sin will continue to have the authority to grip us in its bondage.

Obviously, we must not ignore sin and demonic strongholds in our lives—this is the message of this book. However, once we discover the strongholds in our lives, we must deal with them and overcome them. A religious spirit will keep our attention fixed on the evil at play in our fallen nature instead of on the glory of the Lord and the cross. This spirit is a counterfeit of the true love of God and of true worship.

A religious spirit ensnares its victims into being proud. It keeps us from hearing the voice of God by encouraging us to assume that we already know God's opinion, what He is saying, and what pleases Him. This delusion is the result of believing that God is just like us. It causes us to think rebukes, exhortations, and words of correction that align with Scripture are for other people but not for us. This is why it is vital for us to remain humble and teachable.

A religious spirit can create a zeal that is not pure in motive. Zeal is good, but we must identify *why* we are zealous. The apostle Paul writes in Romans 10:2 concerning the Israelites: "I can testify about them that they are zealous for God, but their zeal is not based on knowledge." Those who are truly zealous for God will become a threat to the enemy, so he will attempt to push their zeal too far by getting them to glory in their own efforts and abilities.

If the enemy can get us to take pride in our gifts and trap us in the lie that we are better and more anointed than others, he will have hooked us in his snare, and we will find ourselves using our gifts with impure motives. Zeal combined with prideful and impure motives is a magnet for a religious spirit to grip our thoughts, emotions, and actions. Thoughts such as, "Wow, God used me more than anyone else tonight in our ministry time"; or, "When we pray for the sick at church, I have seen more people healed than anyone else. I am the most anointed one"; or, "God has blessed me more than the others in my workplace; I am obviously the most gifted" are prideful and religious thoughts that should be taken captive and not entertained. When God's gifts are used powerfully in and through us, we need to stay in a place of humility and thankfulness for the privilege we have to partner with our Lord in blessing others.

Friends, Jesus came to counter a religious spirit. He did not come to bring religion but to bring the kingdom of God. Jesus had great authority over demons and the enemy during His earthly ministry. However, the religious spirit that He countered in the religious leaders of His day was an attitude that grew to a demonic stronghold that ultimately blinded those leaders, hindering their ability to see the promised Messiah when He stood in their midst.

As a result, these zealous religious leaders quickly became Jesus's greatest enemies. No one at this time had prayed more, fasted more, studied more, and had greater hope in the coming Messiah. But sadly, those who were the most zealous for the Word of God opposed the new spiritual season Jesus brought and ended up crucifying the Word Himself when He became flesh among them. We must be on guard to know the motive behind our zeal to ensure that we remain pliable, teachable, and humble. Zeal without the wisdom of the Lord can produce foolishness. We must not become the religious voice that opposes the new, legitimate moves of God.

We must not fall into the trap of always watching and glorifying the work of the enemy in our lives. We are to identify the lies we have believed, repent of our sin, renounce it, receive freedom, and move on. We are to live in the freedom, strength, and peace of heart that Jesus modeled for us. Staying in a place of victimization and of always needing freedom from our sin and guilt is a trap of the religious spirit.

WE WILL LEARN THAT "IT'S NOT ABOUT ME"

Jesus never focused on serving Himself but rather on taking care of others. But in the church today, the continual focus on "me" is becoming a growing issue. Many people choose Christianity because of what they can get out of the Christian walk. While God does absolutely love us and wants to bless us, in order for us to be kingdom-minded, victorious sons and daughters, our focus must be on helping not only ourselves but also others. An outflow of a maturing relationship with the Lord is a desire to reach out and impact others.

As we grow, our prayer and passion become: "God, use me. God, how can I impact others? Lord, use me to extend Your kingdom plan." Not only do we pray this prayer, but we begin to take action to follow God's plan for our lives. A Christian walk is not just about living a good and moral life and waiting to get to heaven but also about becoming a sold-out son or daughter who influences those around us and this world. We should want to leave our mark in the world in the time that we have been blessed with life on this earth. The reality is, when Jesus walked the earth, He modeled for us how we are to influence others.

WE WILL GAIN A KINGDOM PERSPECTIVE

We are to assess and see things the way Jesus sees them. We live in this world, but we are of a kingdom that is not of this world. To have the mind of Christ, we need a shift in our spiritual understanding as to who we are in Christ and what our kingdom position in Him is. We are heirs of God and coheirs with Christ (Rom. 8:17).

The Greek word for *heir* is *kleronomos*, which means "the recipient of divine promises." To be a coheir means that we are fellow or joint receivers with Jesus. We are sons and daughters of God and members of a kingdom family. Our God is not a mean, punitive God sitting on His throne in heaven, wringing His hands out of anger or anxious concern over you and me. He is loving, merciful, gracious, and true. He sees great kingdom potential in all of His children. Scripture tells us that He has made available to us everything that pertains to life and godliness. God has made accessible to each of us all that is necessary for us to live a life that is set apart for His worship and service.

So let's stand in a place of believing the promises of God. As His sons and daughters, we are more than conquerors. Allow the truth of this promise to be established in your thoughts, understanding, emotions, and identity. Choose this day His kingdom, His kingdom perspective, and His righteousness!

We Will Value What Jesus Values

There is no end to the awesomeness of our Savior. We could write multitudes of books and still not touch the fullness of who He is and of the inheritance He has afforded to us. Throughout this book we have discussed many topics that the Lord greatly values. Each of these should matter to us as well if we are going to live full kingdom lives and gain victory over strongholds.

To continue to impart faith in you to pursue the mind of Christ, I have included a comprehensive list of the things Jesus values. Take the attributes of God already discussed in this chapter and your kingdom-identity list from chapter 10, and meditate on them along with the list below. Speak them out loud, and determine to rewire and transform your thought life and your emotions. Fill yourself up with the awesome goodness of our God, and step into His glorious freedom so that you will be empowered to show forth the goodness and value of the King and His kingdom.

What does Jesus value, and what should we value?

- All people, including you and me
- Salvation for all mankind
- His Father
- The Holy Spirit
- His church (His bride)
- Forgiveness
- Compassion
- Grace
- Mercy
- Virtue
- Purity
- His creation
- His kingdom
- Thinking the best of others
- Discernment
- A mind ruled not by confusion and fear but by peace
- A heart ruled not by rejection but by acceptance
- Worship
- His written Word
- His prophetic word and His destiny for our lives
- Deliverance

- Our freedom
- That we have a personal relationship with Him
- Holiness
- Righteousness
- Justice
- Honor
- Healing
- Those things that are lovely
- His good report
- Praise
- Thanksgiving
- Affirmation
- Blessings
- Our kingdom identity
- Enduring faith
- The home and a family life set apart for Him
- Healthy kingdom relationships
- Intimacy
- Authority
- Sound minds
- Wisdom
- Whole and healed emotions
- Seeing Satan's schemes and strongholds defeated

- Faithfulness to prayer
- That we make restitution where it is needed
- Teachable attitudes
- A life of integrity
- Perseverance
- Steadfastness
- Trustworthiness
- Boldness and authority against darkness
- Prophetic destinies being fulfilled

WE WILL RADIATE THE GLORY OF GOD

In closing our journey, I would like to emphasize again what Paul so beautifully stated:

> Whenever, though, they turn to face God as Moses did, God removes the veil and there they are—face-to-face! They suddenly recognize that God is a living, personal presence, not a piece of chiseled stone. And when God is personally present, a living Spirit, that old, constricting legislation is recognized as obsolete. We're free of it! All of us! Nothing between us and God, our faces shining with the brightness of his face. And so we are transfigured much like the Messiah, our lives gradually becoming brighter and more beautiful as God enters our lives and we become like him.
> —2 CORINTHIANS 3:16–18, THE MESSAGE

As we look into God's Word, encounter His presence, and see His Son, the Spirit transforms us into the very image of God. We become alive and truly assured that we are free indeed. We engage in a visible change on the outside that is birthed on the inside. What is the awesome promise of God provided to us in this change? Moses *reflected* the glory of God, but you and I may *radiate* the glory of God. Our lives become brighter and brighter and more beautiful like our Lord Jesus Christ as we grow "from glory to glory."

BREAKING FREE FROM DECEPTION

As we come to a close, I asked a dear friend whom we will refer to as Joy to share her testimony of how the enemy brought deception into her life and how our awesome Lord brought victorious freedom.

> For weeks, as I drove to the gym I continually heard the phrase, "In the end times even the elect would be deceived," which comes from Mark 13:22. I kept thinking God was asking me to pray for one of the national leaders my husband and I are affiliated with in order to ward off an attack of the enemy. It never occurred to me that I might be the one in the process of being caught in a web of deception. Little did I realize the warning was for me.
>
> My husband and I had been in full-time ministry for twelve years and had seen many awesome healings, miracles, deliverances, and salvations. My husband was very involved in several apostolic networks and participated in many strategic spiritual warfare initiatives. I had not participated in those events with him because I felt my calling was more to minister to girls who had been raped and were dealing with post abortive issues (both of which I had experienced in my past). During this time, I was also providing full-time care for my parents, who were living with us. My mom especially needed careful attention because she had dementia/Alzheimer's disease. This caregiving proved to be emotionally taxing on me, and left me tired and vulnerable. Following her death, I slowly stopped being as involved

in ministry activities in order to spend more time with my dad as we grieved the loss of my mother.

I also began going to the gym to deal with the stress in my life. While at the gym, I became acquainted with an individual who shared a keen interest in health and "natural" healing remedies. This man was of Jewish lineage, and I have had a deep love for Israel since I was a child, so I reasoned that perhaps God had brought about this friendship in order for me to witness to him. During our conversations, he shared that he was also a Reiki master teacher and he talked about being a very spiritual person. Reiki is a Japanese/Buddhist spiritual practice that involves stress reduction and relaxation. The practitioner will lay hands on a person and release the energy of the "higher power" and the "life force energy."

I started doing some research on Reiki, and for every website I found that called Reiki occultic, I found one that said Reiki and Christian beliefs could be complementary. Of course, I gravitated toward the thought that Reiki would enhance my spiritual life and continued investigating it along with transcendental meditation. I asked this individual about doing a liver cleanse, as cleanses are all the rage in health clubs. He provided me with an Ayurvedic potion (a cleanse that is associated with Hindu beliefs and practices), which I purposed to do while my husband was out of town. I lied to my husband, telling him I would not do the liver cleanse while he was gone, but the truth was that I had already started it. Meanwhile, my husband was attending a commissioning service, where an apostolic prayer ministry was setting him in place as an apostle over a larger area.

While doing this cleanse associated with Hindu beliefs, I was caught in total deception! Or more accurately, I had allowed myself to come under the power of a spirit of deception. In the ensuing days and weeks, I found myself doing things that I would *never* have done before—lying to my husband, buying burner phones so I could communicate with this man, sexting with him, questioning all my beliefs about my faith, and listening to music I had never even liked before. I went from a woman who loved the Lord and my husband with all my heart to someone who was telling her husband she wanted a divorce! I was willing to sacrifice everything I held dear—my faith, my marriage, my family, our animals—everything!

Needless to say, my husband was blindsided by all that was occurring with his wife. The Holy Spirit had prompted him to question my time at the gym, and he repeatedly asked to go with me. I politely said I didn't want to waste his time, as my routine was longer than his (all a cover-up for the time I was spending talking to this other man). He asked key leaders to pray for us and even stepped back from many of the organizations he held leadership positions with in order to minister to and fight for me. The Holy Spirit would continually tell him where I was, what I was doing, and where to find the phones I kept purchasing and hiding. As hard as the enemy of my soul was fighting to have me, the Holy Spirit was helping my husband to fight for my very soul!

When I finally reached a breaking point, the Lord told me to reach out to Becca and ask for her help in deliverance and prayer. The night after I set an appointment with Becca, when I drifted off to sleep, my husband saw the sheets covering me begin to move. Because I had asked for help, he knew he could cast the spirit of deception out of me, which he did. I actually don't remember that happening, but I mark that night as the time when I began realizing the depth of the deception I had entered into.

I was devastated as I realized that I had allowed the enemy to destroy my relationships with Jesus and my husband, the ministry God had so richly blessed us with, our influence in our region, our finances, and even those around us. The deception was so strong that everyone on our ministry leadership team also came under the spirit of deception, and many relationships were destroyed. Every area of our lives was impacted in a manner that to this day causes me great sadness.

I rededicated my life to Jesus, and my husband and I renewed our marriage vows and began the restoration process. As I look back on that period of time, I marvel to see the hand of God ordering and directing our steps. The pain of realizing all the enemy was able to do in such a short period of time, and the devastation he wrought, will probably always be with me. However, I know I am forgiven and that Jesus has set me free from all the chains that ensnared me. God so wonderfully told us what to do at each stage of the recovery process—from going through personal deliverance ministry and repenting of and renouncing the lies I had believed to being water baptized again by my husband. I captured *every* thought that was not from God, and I filled my mind with the Word, listened to anointed preaching, and prayed in the Spirit. And my husband and I committed to open and honest communication with each other, even when it was very difficult to do.

I clearly remember the day I heard the Lord tell me that He had created me to worship Him. It was the first time I had heard Him speak that clearly in months, and I was undone! I think I cried for hours, and I haven't stopped worshipping Him in song and deed since! I have fallen so deeply in love with my

Jesus and will spend the rest of my life talking about Him, and His faithfulness and goodness!

My desire in sharing my story is to help open people's eyes to how cunning and sly the deceiver is and how *great* our God is! My husband and I are now beginning to re-enter ministry as the Lord brings opportunities for us to be used as sharp threshing instruments!

Why do I share this story? To encourage each of you reading this book that no matter where you have come from, what you are struggling with, or the battle that you are contending with in your thoughts and emotions, God can and will set you free! There is no scheme of the enemy; no stronghold of the mind; no lie, deception, or emotional struggle that is more powerful than the love of our heavenly Father, the blood of Jesus, and the all-consuming presence of the Holy Spirit. This is your day to truly defeat strongholds of the mind and live in victorious freedom. As Jesus promises in His Word, "So if the Son liberates you [makes you free men], then you are really and unquestionably free" (John 8:36, AMP).

LET'S PRAY TO HAVE THE MIND OF CHRIST

Father, thank You for touching my life and setting me free from the strongholds that have gripped my mind and emotions. You are an awesome, faithful, delivering God, and I rejoice that the strongholds in my mind and emotions have been defeated!

I choose this day to encounter the mind of Christ. God, cause me to love what You love and to lead a lifestyle of love, compassion, holiness, humility, patience, and faithfulness. Lord, I commit to live a life based on Your truth, love, and grace. Cause me to hate evil and sin. Keep me from evil and its temptations. Holy Spirit, fill me up to overflowing. May I walk freely in Your Spirit and welcome a new move of Your love, anointing, grace, and authority to flow through my life. Teach me to live life abiding in Your presence. Lord, I declare that from this day forward I will value what You value and live a victorious life as Your child. I delight in the truth that You have called me out of darkness and into Your marvelous light. Lord, I choose to take refuge in You. I choose to be glad and to sing for joy.

Spread Your protection over me. I love You and rejoice in Your name. Lord, bless me and surround me with Your favor as a shield. May I behold and experience You in new ways. I desire more of You, Jesus. Cause me to be transformed from glory to glory into Your image and to be a child that radiates You. In Jesus's name I pray, amen.

APPENDIX

I HAVE INCLUDED A list of witchcraft, occult, and cult activities that can prove to be an open door allowing the enemy to establish strongholds in our minds. As discussed in chapter 6, our possessions and our entertainment choices reveal our priorities. If we have opened ourselves up to ungodly practices or beliefs, or still possess objects from these activities, they can be a red-carpet invitation for confusion and torment.

Keep in mind that this is not an exhaustive list, but it will prove to be a good starting point to help you know what unholy practices to avoid and to rid your home of. I have given definitions and descriptions to several practices that need further clarification than what was provided earlier in this book.

I am often asked how are we to know or discern what is an acceptable practice and what is not. My first response or counsel is that we must pray and seek the Lord. My second word of advice is that we should research the history of what we are choosing to engage in. If the practice is demonic, idolatrous, and unbiblical at its foundation, then I say it is something we should not embrace. God is looking for a church that is holy, without compromise, and not so conformed to the culture that we "fit into it without even thinking" (Rom. 12:1, THE MESSAGE).

FREEMASONRY

In our deliverance ministry we consistently pray for people who have personally been involved in Freemasonry or whose ancestors were actively part of this fraternal society. On the surface Freemasonry appears to be a reputable organization. Membership involves, for instance, generous contributions to reputable charitable institutions. Additionally, many historical figures have been active Freemasons. But the unfortunate truth is that Freemasonry has demonic roots.

The origins of this "secret society" is rooted in the worship of Osiris, Isis, and Hors, pagan gods of ancient Egypt. All the tenets within this group are derived from the worship of these demon gods.

Freemasonry endorses the Luciferian doctrine that Satan is just as evil as God is good—meaning that the enemy is as powerful as our heavenly Father. It teaches that men become gods. It forbids discussing or sharing the Christian faith in meetings. All members are free to worship the deity of their choice and are told that whatever god they worship is the true way to eternal life. To help guide us in this discussion, read the following quote pointing to Freemasons' belief in pagan gods. It is taken from *Morals and Dogma* by Albert Pike, who served as the Sovereign Grand Commander of the Freemasons' Ancient and Accepted Scottish Rite, Southern Jurisdiction, in 1859. It discusses the Knight of the Brazen Serpent Degree:

> This Degree is both philosophical and moral. While it teaches the necessity of reformation as well as repentance, as a means of obtaining mercy and forgiveness, it is also devoted to an explanation of the symbols of Masonry; and especially to those which are connected with that ancient and universal legend, of which that of Khir-Om Abi is but a variation; that legend which, representing a murder or a death, and a restoration to life, by a drama in which figure Osiris, Isis and Horus, Atys and Cybele, Adonis and Venus, the Cabiri, Dionusos, and many another representative of the active and passive Powers of Nature, taught the Initiates in the Mysteries that the rule of Evil and

> Darkness is but temporary, and that that of Light and
> Good will be eternal.[1]

I realize that this might be uncomfortable for some people to read. To help further guide you in understanding more about the beliefs of Freemasons, I recommend *Masonry: Beyond the Light* by William Schnoebelen and *Unmasking Freemasonry—Removing the Hoodwink* by Selwyn Stevens. Another great resource is *Free From Freemasonry* written by Ron Campbell. The book is out of print, but you can still find copies on Amazon.

MARTIAL ARTS

As I travel and teach about overcoming strongholds, I find that some people resist the idea that martial arts grew out of Buddhism and Taoism. Still, it is true. A pagan religious heritage exists at the core of these fighting sports. The *Dictionary of Cults, Sects, Religions, and the Occult* gives this insight:

> The religious significance of the arts lies in the harmonizing of life forces (Yin and Yang) and the ability to harness "Ch'i" [universal energy]. Masters in the martial arts accomplish tremendous physical feats. The ability to strike or kick with tremendous physical force or to smash a pile of bricks with a single blow is attributed to "Ch'i."[2]

Martial arts such as aikido, judo, jujitsu, karate, kung fu, Ninjitsu, ta'i chi Ch'uan, tae kwon do, and numerous others do have pagan and ungodly roots. I have known people who have dealt with intense spirits of anger and violence because of participation in martial arts. If we open ourselves to something with demonic roots, even if we do it unknowingly, strongholds still have access to our thoughts and emotions.

I have heard the argument that God can make the martial arts pure, meaning that Christians can participate in an abridged version of the activity without fear of negative spiritual or emotional effects. I do not believe that God is concerned with making the martial arts pure. If something started as a pagan religion or practice, then it remains a pagan religion or practice. That being said, self-defense and physical fitness activities are not sin in themselves. My challenge to those who are involved in martial arts is to start a self-defense class separate from the structure of martial arts, and one that does not involve the universal ch'i. The Lord tells us in Scripture that we are to keep ourselves pure and holy. We are to be separate and consecrated from the practices of the world and the enemy.

YOGA

The word yoga, meaning "to yoke," comes from the Sanskrit language. Yoga is a Hindu system of philosophy, meditation, and worship of pagan gods. Here is Webster's definition:

> A Hindu theistic philosophy teaching the suppression of all activity of body, mind, and will in order that the self may realize its distinction from them and attain liberation; a system of exercises for attaining bodily or mental control and well-being.[3]

The whole system of these exercises is derived from the worship of Eastern deities. Each yoga position is one of worship to a demonic Hindu god. Numerous Christians attend and even teach yoga classes without fully comprehending the fact that they are opening their souls to spirits of error, confusion, unbelief, antichrist, and witchcraft.

I realize that many of you will not appreciate the above information. I find it ironic that as believers we will spend money on organic vegetables, water purifiers, and all-natural products in order to protect our physical bodies from pollutants and toxins—and we will go to great lengths to show our displeasure when local stores promote immoral products on their shelves—yet we will engage in and oftentimes try to justify our involvement in practices such as Freemasonry, martial arts, and yoga. Friends, our spiritual condition should be an uncompromising priority. We need to know what doors we are opening into our souls.

ADDITIONAL PRACTICES AND ITEMS TO AVOID

- Altered states of consciousness
- Amulets
- Animal sacrifices
- Ascended Masters
- Astral projection
- Astrology
- Auras
- Avatar
- Baha'i faith
- Biofeedback
- Black magic
- Blood subscription
- Buddhism
- Centering
- Chakras
- Channeling
- Charms
- Christian Science

- Clairvoyance
- Crystal balls
- Crystals
- Cybele worship
- DeMolay
- Divination
- Divining rods
- Eastern religions and all objects attached to these religions
- Order of the Eastern Star
- ESP
- Fantasy role-playing games steeped in witchcraft, perversion, and violence
- Feng shui
- Fetishes
- Fortune-telling and all tools used in this practice
- Geomancy
- Goddess worship
- Hare Krishna
- Harry Potter (film and book series)
- Hinduism
- Horoscopes
- Hypnotism
- Idolatry

- Initiation ceremonies centered on pagan and demonic activities
- Iridology
- Islam
- Jehovah's Witnesses
- Job's Daughters
- Kaballah
- Karma
- Koran
- Ku Klux Klan
- Kundalini empowerment, meditation, and worship
- "Light as a feather" levitation game
- Love magic and all items used to cast spells
- Macumba
- Magic
- Mantras
- Martial arts
- Mediumism
- Mind-altering drugs
- Mind-control practices
- Mormonism
- Necromancy
- New Age cults
- New Age meditations
- Numerology

- Occult movies
- Omens
- Ouija boards
- Palm reading
- Parapsychology
- Pentagram
- Pokémon
- Poltergeist
- Psychic power
- Pyramid power
- Rebirthing
- Reiki
- Reincarnation
- Rosary beads
- Rosicrucianism
- Santeria
- Satanic rock music
- Satanism
- Scientology
- Séances
- Shamanism
- Shinto
- Sorcery
- Spirit guides
- Superstition

- Talisman
- Taoism
- Tarot cards
- Tea-leaf reading
- Telepathy
- Twilight (film and book series)
- Unitarianism
- Vampirism and its practices
- Voodoo
- Water witching
- Werewolves
- White magic
- Wicca
- Witchcraft and all objects associated with it
- Yoga
- Zen
- Zodiac

To end on an encouraging note, for years our ministry has witnessed individuals supernaturally healed in their physical bodies, thoughts, and emotions when they repented of and renounced their involvement in these activities. Many who have walked in great mental confusion and torment have received great freedom. We have seen physical and emotional conditions such as heart disease, chronic body pain, allergies, clogged arteries, kidney disease, chronic migraine headaches, depression, and unbelief healed.

NOTES

CHAPTER 1—HOLY SPIRIT, DOES MY MIND NEED FREEDOM?

1. Susan Reynolds, "Happy Brain, Happy Life: Happy Brains are More Creative, Quicker, and More Mentally Alert," *Psychology Today*, August 2, 2011, http://www.psychologytoday.com/blog/prime-your-gray-cells/201108/happy-brain-happy-life (accessed September 9, 2013).

CHAPTER 4—HOW THOUGHTS AFFECT OUR EMOTIONS

1. Mark C. Crowley, *Lead From the Heart: Transformational Leadership in the 21st Century* (New York: Balboa Press, 2011), 41.

2. Noel and Phyl Gibson, *Evicting Demonic Intruders: Guidelines for Pastors and Counsellors on Ministering Freedom to Oppressed Christians* (West Sussex, England: New Wine, 1993), 142.

3. Anxiety and Depression Association of America, "Facts & Statistics," http://www.adaa.org/about-adaa/press-room/facts-statistics (accessed September 10, 2014).

4. Anxiety and Depression Association of America, "Depression," http://www.adaa.org/understanding-anxiety/depression (accessed November 6, 2014).

5. Anxiety and Depression Association of America, "Facts & Statistics."

6. *Merriam-Webster's 11th Collegiate Dictionary* (Springfield MA: Merriam-Webster Incorporated, 2003), s.v. "worry."

CHAPTER 6—HEALING THE MIND FROM THE SCARS OF THE PAST

1. Christy Matta, "How Trauma Can Affect Your Body & Mind," PsychCentral, *World of Psychology* (blog) http://psychcentral.com/blog/archives/2013/04/18/how-trauma-can-affect-your-body-mind/ (accessed September 17, 2014).

2. *Merriam-Webster's 11th Collegiate Dictionary*, s.v. "trauma."

CHAPTER 8—SPEAK WORDS OF LIFE AND BLESSING

1. Science 2.0, "Do Women Really Talk More Than Men?," July 5, 2007, http://www.science20.com/news/do_women_really_talk_more_than_men (accessed October 9, 2013).

2. As cited in Patricia Noll, *Good Me* (New York: Morgan James Publishing, 2014), 161.

3. Barbara Markway, "Stop Fighting Your Negative Thoughts," May 7, 2013, http://www.psychologytoday.com/blog/shyness-is-nice/201305/stop-fighting-your-negative-thoughts (accessed September 13, 2014).

Chapter 9—Resolve to Walk in Freedom

1. Cindy Jacobs, *Possessing the Gates of the Enemy: A Training Manual for Militant Intercession* (Grand Rapids, MI: Chosen, 2009), 95.

Chapter 10—Think on What Is Good

1. Ralph Waldo Emerson as quoted in Stephen R. Covey, *The 7 Habits of Highly Effective People: Powerful Lessons in Personal Change* (New York: RosettaBooks, 2013).

2. *Lee John Drow* (blog), "Fear How Bad Is It?," July 15, 2013, http://leejohndrow.com/fear-how-bad-it-is/ (accessed November 5, 2014); Melissa Marie, "Overcoming Anxiety, Stress and Worry," July 13, 2010, http://www.huckleberryprairie.com/overcoming-anxiety-stress-and-worry (accessed November 5, 2014).

3. As cited in Steven Ungerleider, *Mental Training for Peak Performance* (Emmaus, PA: Rodale, 2005).

Chapter 11—But We Have the Mind of Christ

1. Andrew Murray, *Humility* (New Kingston, PA: Whitaker, 1982), 51.

Appendix

1. Albert Pike, *Morals and Dogma* (Charleston: L. H. Jenkins, Inc., 1950), 435.

2. George A. Mather, Larry A. Nichols, *Dictionary of Cults, Sects, Religions, and the Occult* (Grand Rapids, MI: Zondervan, 1993), 172.

3. Merriam-Webster Online, s.v. "yoga," http://www.merriam-webster.com/dictionary/yoga (accessed September 17, 2014).

AUTHOR'S PAGE

Rebecca is cofounder and president of Christian Harvest International and Strategic Prayer Action Network (SPAN).

Her passion has been seeing the lands of the world impacted for the glory of God, reaching people with the gospel, and setting the captives free. Her heart cry has become, "Lord, give me the nations." As a result, prophecy, prophetic intercession, transformational spiritual warfare prayer, spiritual mapping, deliverance, and teaching the Word of God extensively in the many lands of the earth are the main thrusts of Christian Harvest.

Over the past twenty-two years, she has participated in and led spiritual warfare prayer journeys to twenty-five countries, including Egypt, Nepal, Italy, Turkey, Russia, Ukraine, Ireland, Spain, and China. She also has been involved in prayer journeys to many cities across the United States. Measurable breakthroughs of transformation have been realized as a result.

Having a heart for lost souls, Rebecca has seen many saved and set free. She ministers in transparency from her personal experiences of overcoming fear, depression, and rebellion to walk in freedom. She is committed to equipping people with scriptural truths for how to live an overcoming life of purpose, fulfillment, and destiny, and to help individuals and churches have a Jesus captivated and authoritative prayer life through which change and transformation are realized.

She is the author of six books:

- *Authority to Tread: An Intercessor's Guide to Strategic-Level Spiritual Warfare*
- *Breaking the Bonds of Evil: How to Set People Free From Demonic Oppression*
- *The Power of a Godly Mother* (ebook)
- *Destined to Rule: Spiritual Strategies for Advancing the Kingdom of God*
- *Let Our Children Go: Steps to Free Your Child From Evil Influence and Demonic Harassment*
- *Your Kingdom Come: Encouraged to Intercede*
- *Understanding Spiritual Warfare: Four Views* (an academic book discussing four theological views of spiritual warfare, which will be used in seminaries throughout the United States)
- *Defeating Strongholds of the Mind*

While she loves to travel the world and partner with the Lord in touching people's lives, Rebecca's favorite and most cherished times are with her husband, Greg, and their three beautiful daughters, Kendall, Rebecca, and Katie. They reside in Colorado Springs, Colorado, and are members of Freedom Church.

Rebecca has been a guest on TBN, Sid Roth's *It's Supernatural!*, *God Knows*, and *The Harvest Show*. She has written for publications such as *Charisma*, *Pray!*, and *Spirit-Led Woman* magazines. She graduated with a doctorate of practical ministry from Wagner Leadership Institute, where she also serves as a core faculty member.

All of her materials are available through her office at 719-243-3302 or at www.christianharvestintl.org. If you are interested in inviting Mrs. Greenwood to speak at your church or event, contact her office or e-mail chi@christianharvestintl.org.

FREE YOUR CHILDREN FROM
DEMONIC HARASSMENT
AND TEACH THEM TO STAY FREE!

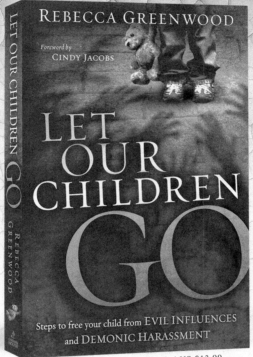

ISBN: 978-1-61638-258-2 I US $13.99

Let Our Children Go is a handbook for parents, pastors, and leaders to help free children from evil influences and demonic harassment. You will learn how to:

- Determine if an evil spirit is harassing a child
- Deal with demonic influences and harassment when they occur
- Train children to identify demonic activity and eliminate it from their lives

CHARISMA
HOUSE

12929

WWW.CHARISMAHOUSE.COM

SUBSCRIBE TODAY

Exclusive Content

Inspiring Messages

Encouraging Articles

Discovering Freedom

CHARISMA MEDIA

FREE NEWSLETTERS

to experience the power of the *Holy Spirit*

Charisma Magazine Newsletter
Get top-trending articles, Christian teachings, entertainment reviews, videos, and more.

Charisma News Weekly
Get the latest breaking news from an evangelical perspective every Monday.

SpiritLed Woman
Receive amazing stories, testimonies, and articles on marriage, family, prayer, and more.

New Man
Get articles and teaching about the realities of living in the world today as a man of faith.

3-in-1 Daily Devotionals
Find personal strength and encouragement with these devotionals, and begin your day with God's Word.

Sign up for Free at nl.charismamag.com